SUCCESSFUL GARDENING

SUCCESSFUL
GARDENING

David Carr

BLACK CAT

The publishers would like to thank the following individuals and organisations for their kind permission to reproduce the illustrations in this book:

Bernard Alfieri; Heather Angel; A-Z Collection; Barnaby's Picture Library; Ken Beckett; Brecht-Einzig Ltd; Butterfly Building Materials Ltd; Celuform Ltd; Cement & Concrete Association; Bruce Coleman; R. J. Corbin; John Cowley; P. Craig; Brian M. Fuller; Brian Furner; A. du Gard Pasley; Iris Hardwick; Bill Heritage; Angelo Hornack; Hozelock; G. E. Hyde; I.C.I.; E. A. James/ NHPA; Marley Buildings Ltd; Tania Midgeley; Ken Muir; Orbis, Eric Crichton, John Glover, Jerry Harpur, John Heseltine, Kim Sayer; Penrhyn Quarries; Photographic Collection; Photos Horticultural; Roy Proctor; Max Rothmore; Donald Smith; Harry Smith Horticultural Collection; A. South; Stapeley Water Gardens; P. Stiles; Tony Store; Suttons Seeds; Tinsley Wire Company; Michael Warren; Wolf Ltd; Womans Own.

First published in Great Britain 1985 by
Orbis Publishing Limited 1985
Reprinted 1989 by Macdonald & Co
(Publishers) Ltd
under the Black Cat imprint

Macdonald & Co (Publishers) Ltd,
Headway House,
66-73 Shoe Lane,
London EC4P 4AB

a member of Maxwell Pergamon
Publishing Corporation plc

ISBN 0-7481-0206-X
Printed in Italy

CONTENTS

FIRST STEPS

Make gardening fun. Once you've written out your basic needs and preliminary ideas, do some investigating to see what others in similar circumstances have achieved. Look through magazines and good gardening books. Seek out any flower shows and nurseries or garden centres large enough to display model gardens. Don't allow yourself to be overly influenced by those around you. But, at the same time, be receptive to local knowledge – this can prove invaluable.

As your 'research' continues and your ideas become more firmly established, you may begin to surprise yourself as your own preferences emerge. You may even find you have a flair for planning. By following the advice in this chapter you can avoid many mistakes, frustrations – and unnecessary expense.

What do you want from your garden?

If you are looking for ideas to include in the layout of a new garden, or you are about to consider making alterations to an existing one, 'Successful Gardening' can help. It is designed to guide you through, systematically and in easy stages, from planning and planting to aftercare. The basic know-how is set out in a practical, easy to grasp manner. Ways to save time and needless expense, and how to avoid common mistakes, are also pinpointed. Colourful and attractive gardens don't come about by chance – careful planning and attention to detail are needed.

You may have moved house. Perhaps your present garden is not entirely to your liking aesthetically or is a bit unmanageable. You may be faced with the job of laying out a new garden. Regardless of whether you are starting from scratch or contemplating alterations, take time to decide what you want and what suits your needs. The pipe dream of a neat layout, with masses of colourful and fragrant flowers, a deep green lawn – maybe water sparkling in warm sunlight, while you relax on the patio – is perhaps not so far away as you imagine.

Colour Colour is high on the list of priorities for most people. Colour schemes are largely a matter of personal taste and also of trial and error. Strong warm colours – reds, yellows, oranges and shocking pinks – can brighten up dull areas, or enliven a patio or court-yard. Blues, grey-greens and pastels, the so-called cool colours, help to create an illusion of distance, and can look attractive used as a background. A green or grey hedge provides an excellent foil for colourful flowers. Blue with white; red with yellow or orange; and pink with purple can all prove to be attractive colour combinations. Simple schemes are usually more successful and

easier to implement than the more elaborate ones. Consider, for example, exploiting various shades of one colour.

Season of interest If you want to avoid a bare, drab garden in winter, plant plenty of conifer and other evergreens. Don't forget that foliage colour can be as brilliant as flowers. The crimson, flame, orange and yellow autumn leaf tints of many trees and shrubs are quite spectacular. Here maples excel. Berried shrubs too give valuable autumn and winter colour.

Bedding plants, along with border perennials, are unrivalled for providing eye-catching splashes of colour from spring until autumn – depending on variety and treatment. As well as in the open ground, there is plenty of scope for colourful plants grown up walls and in containers – even between paving slabs!

Instant effects Newly laid out gardens, in which young shrubs are set out at recommended spacings, tend to look flat for the first few years. This is due to the wide expanse of bare soil. An instant, mature effect is possible by planting a few older, container-grown trees and shrubs, which adds considerably to the cost; by close planting of smaller shrubs, which must be thinned before they become overcrowded; or, finally, by interplanting the permanent shrubs with quick-growing, less expensive fillers. Herbaceous border plants and annuals are useful for the purpose, but, again, they must be removed in good time.

Style Decide whether you prefer to have a formal garden, laid out on symmetrical lines, or an informal one. This is largely a matter of personal taste, but formal gardens are generally easier to design and lay out, provided you are dealing with a regularly shaped area. Try to avoid the stiffness of straight lines in an informal garden. Introduce loosely curved edges to round off

Gardens can be shaped to suit varying needs and lifestyles. Some may prefer a slightly woodsy effect, such as that shown (left), with its profusion of Sweet William. A patio area (above top) makes the garden a very real extension of the home; and a 'children's garden' (above) allows young children to play freely – and safely.

corners of beds and lawns. Planting between paving slabs and allowing plants to grow over the paving in some places helps break up straight lines.

There is nothing wrong with having a formal area within an informal garden, especially near the house, where the symmetrical lines of a patio can complement the architecture. Hard surfaces in general tend to be most successful when treated formally.

Function and layout Draw up a priority list of what you would like to see in your garden, and what you are likely to use or need. Consider a patio, lawn, beds and borders, vegetable patch, garden frame, greenhouse, rock garden or garden pool, and somewhere for the children and pets to play. Do be selective and don't fall into the trap of deciding you are going to have everything, especially if your garden is on the small side.

Practical considerations When making up your list don't overlook the essentials like paths, drives, drying areas and somewhere for household as well as garden waste. You are likely to want a garden that is easily managed, without too much time, expense and effort involved. The garden also needs to be safe for children, the elderly and pets. Ways and means of achieving these ends are discussed later.

Weighing up your site

Many people make the mistake of pushing ahead with making or improving their garden without first giving enough thought to the garden's full potential – and to its limitations. Many is the time you see trees and shrubs which have hopelessly outgrown the available space. To avoid this, and other similar problems, take a hard look at the site before you begin. And while you are about it, jot down notes and ideas – you can't commit everything to memory. Later on, these notes will come in handy when you start to plan the layout.

Site conditions, location and climate If you garden in the harsh conditions of the north of Britain, where winters are hard and long, the choice of outdoor plants is going to be restricted. By comparison, southern and south-western areas have relatively short, mild winters – especially in those districts near the coast. These favoured areas have longer growing seasons than the north. As a rough guide, the growing season is

This lovely garden (right) is the result of careful planning, analysis of site and soil, some hard work and several years of nurturing the whole thing as it developed and matured from the original base plot of land (below).

delayed by about a week for every 160km (100 miles) further north you live.

For practical purposes, we have broadly grouped gardens into three regions: northern, central and southern. Choose your plants to suit.

Shelter and aspect Any garden, if open and exposed to chilling or drying winds, will be cold and difficult. Winds from the north and east can be devastating. The warmest and most favoured positions in the garden are those against a south-facing wall – or on a sunny south-facing slope, sheltered from cold prevailing winds. In descending order of warmth are west-facing walls, fences and banks; followed by east-facing aspects; finally finishing up with the north-facing colder positions. Beds only a few paces away from a warm wall are generally a great deal cooler than

those at the foot of the wall. East-facing sites, exposed to early morning sun, are not for conifers and evergreens. Frozen leaves and buds tend to thaw out too quickly and become damaged in consequence.

Light and shade Many garden plants have quite definite preferences for full sun, while others may need partial shade. Some will tolerate permanent shade. To help match plant needs with site conditions, assess the light levels in your garden, and divide it into sunny, semi-shaded, and shaded areas. South-facing positions, unshaded by trees, structures or buildings, receive most sun. The east-facing side of a wall gets morning sun with afternoon shade. The west side gets morning shade and afternoon sun. Beds under fully leaved trees, and on north sides of buildings, are normally in permanent shade.

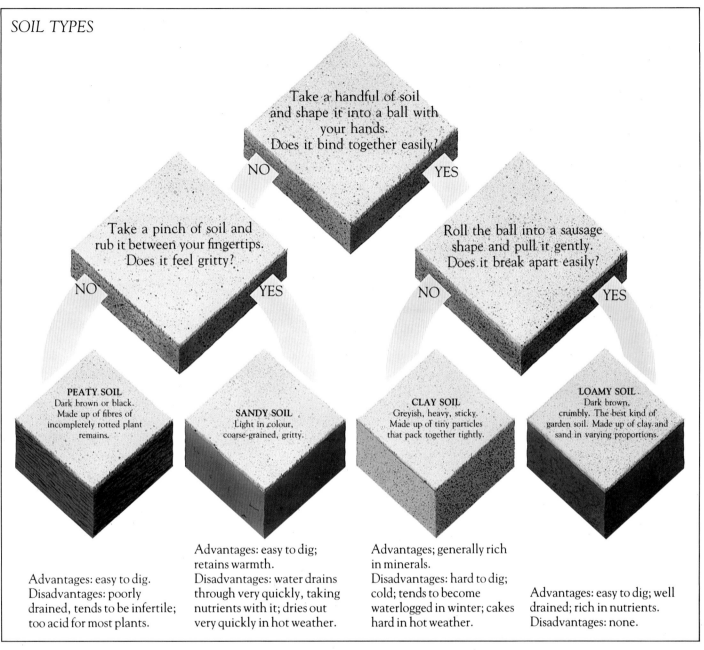

SOIL TYPES

Take a handful of soil and shape it into a ball with your hands. Does it bind together easily?

NO   YES

Take a pinch of soil and rub it between your fingertips. Does it feel gritty?

NO   YES

Roll the ball into a sausage shape and pull it gently. Does it break apart easily?

NO   YES

PEATY SOIL
Dark brown or black. Made up of fibres of incompletely rotted plant remains.

SANDY SOIL
Light in colour, coarse-grained, gritty.

CLAY SOIL
Greyish, heavy, sticky. Made up of tiny particles that pack together tightly.

LOAMY SOIL
Dark brown, crumbly. The best kind of garden soil. Made up of clay and sand in varying proportions.

Advantages: easy to dig. Disadvantages: poorly drained, tends to be infertile; too acid for most plants.

Advantages: easy to dig; retains warmth. Disadvantages: water drains through very quickly, taking nutrients with it; dries out very quickly in hot weather.

Advantages; generally rich in minerals. Disadvantages: hard to dig; cold; tends to become waterlogged in winter; cakes hard in hot weather.

Advantages: easy to dig; well drained; rich in nutrients. Disadvantages: none.

Soil

You need to know what kind of soil exists in your garden if you are to avoid mistakes in cultivation, planting and aftercare. Garden soil is made up of mineral particles of various size; organic matter, composed mainly of decaying vegetation with microbes and other forms of soil life; soil air in the spaces between soil particles; and, finally, there is the constituent so easily taken for granted – soil moisture.

Texture The mineral particles and organic matter content provide the clues to soil type. The mineral content is composed of varying amounts of stones, sand and clay.

A few simple tests will help you decide what kind of soil you have. First, take a good look at the soil surface, when cleared of weeds and rubbish. If the surface is stony, with numerous pebbles over 1cm (½in) in diameter, the soil will burn up badly in summer. Peaty soil is very dark, spongy to the touch and fibrous. It contains a high

proportion of partially decayed organic matter, can be acid and needs generous feeding. If the soil surface is fairly dark, becoming increasingly light coloured when you dig down, your soil is likely to contain lime. If, after visually assessing your soil, you are in doubt, do a chemical soil test; it can be very important if you are growing lime-sensitive plants.

If your soil doesn't seem to fit the descriptions, test a handful of moist earth. If the soil feels gritty and is mid-brown or grey-brown, then it's sandy. This is free draining, hungry soil. If the

soil feels sticky, is greasy, leaves a shiny smear, and dries to a hard lump or fine dust, your soil is heavy clay. This is a very difficult, slow-draining soil which bakes hard and cracks when dry. If your soil is dark brown and not really sticky, yet when wet will squeeze into a ball which shatters easily if dropped, you have loam soil. It is an ideal soil in which most garden plants will thrive.

Drainage Good drainage is essential if plants are to have a healthy, flourishing root system. If water lies on the surface for long periods after rain has stopped, the soil is waterlogged and needs draining. However, it is not always obvious from the surface that drainage is poor. You can check this during winter by digging a trial hole. Make it about 30cm (12in) square, and 45cm (18in) deep, choosing a low-lying position. Cover the hole, to keep out rain; the dustbin lid will do, provided it is weighted down. Inspect the hole regularly, particularly after rain, tightly replacing the cover each time. If water rises to within 20cm (8in) of the surface or nearer, you need to improve soil drainage.

Sometimes poor drainage and stunted plant growth are due to a hard compacted layer, or hard pan, in the top 45cm (18in) of soil. This can easily be determined by digging down with a spade. Drainage and soils are discussed in Chapter 5.

Soil fertility The tests previously discussed relate to the texture of the soil. Now consider the chemical side of soil fertility. Soils can be tested for their nutrient content – the amount of nitrogen, phosphate and potash present. This testing allows for greater precision in manuring and feeding. Provided plants are healthy and doing well, and are fed occasionally, testing for nutrients

is not generally considered essential, and certainly not routine practice. However, if you have reason to doubt the fertility of your soil, then do a test, allowing plenty of time before sowing or planting to correct any deficiencies.

When it comes to checking lime content, it is accepted practice to test soils more frequently. If you are growing lime-sensitive plants, test the soil once every two or three years because plant health is closely linked with lime levels in the soil. Low lime content encourages diseases like the dreaded club root among members of the cabbage family. Too much lime results in lime haters like rhododendrons developing chlorosis, and potatoes becoming infected with scab. Testing can take place at any time, but autumn or winter is usually best, since this is the ideal time to apply lime. Lime content is expressed as pH; pH7 is neutral, above is alkaline and below is acid.

Taking soil samples Remove a tablespoonful of soil from at least five or six different spots in the garden. Take the soil from the root zone, which is about 10-15cm (4-6in) below the surface, each time removing any stones, roots and hard lumps. Crumble the soil, and mix thoroughly on a clean plastic sheet. This soil is then ready for testing and constitutes one sample. If you have a big garden, then repeat the process several times. Sampling needs to be carried out with care if the test results are to be meaningful.

Methods of testing You can obtain a detailed analysis of your soil by sending samples to a laboratory for testing. This can prove quite expensive, and is norm-

The fact that everything in this neglected garden – including the weeds – is a healthy green is a sign that the soil is a good one.

SOIL TESTING

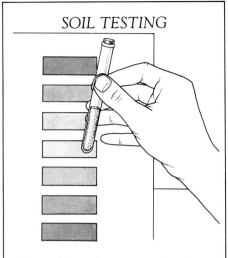

Place soil from the top 15cm (6in) into each test tube. Follow with reagent, cork and shake. When the contents settle, compare the colours with those on the charts for pH value and mineral levels.

ally only resorted to when serious soil problems arise. Some garden centres and fertilizer firms also test soil.

For average purposes, a DIY soil test kit enables you to test your soil quickly and easily at home. These kits are advertised in the gardening press and are available from most garden centres and stores. If used sensibly, most kits provide sufficiently accurate results. They come complete with full instructions. Basically, a portion of soil sample is put in a test tube. Reagent (chemical) is poured in, the tube is stoppered and shaken vigorously. After the mixture settles, the colour of the liquid in the tube is compared with the colour on a chart, and the resulting comparison indicates pH values or nutrient levels.

Test meters Both pH meters and soil fertility meters are available. Metal probes are pushed into the soil and the results appear on a simple dial. There is no need to take soil samples, as meters are normally used directly in the border soil. Unfortunately, unless you buy one of the more expensive models, the results may be far from accurate.

Symbols for plant needs

The following symbols are used in Chapter 6, which deals with choosing plants. The symbols follow the plant names and are a shorthand system detailing the plant's main requirements.

Hardiness
H = Hardy. It can be grown outdoors for the duration of its useful life.
HH = Half-hardy. Not frost hardy. It may need indoor protection over winter, or starting off in warmth.
G = Greenhouse/indoor plant. It needs protection all year round.

Space needs
Ht = Height. Headroom needed.
Sp = Spacing. Distance apart.

Light needs
○ = Full sun
◑ = Semi- or partial shade
● = Tolerant of permanent light shade

Soil needs (preference/tolerance)
A = Acid soil
C = Chalky/lime-rich soil
N = Neutral soil

Treatment and type of plant
a = Annual. Start from seed each year. It flowers and dies within twelve months.
B = Biennial. Sow one year to flower and die the following year.
P = Perennial. Plant out to flower year after year.
  Note: There are some perennials which are better treated as annuals, and some better treated as biennials.
Sh = Shrub ⎫
Cl = Climber ⎬ Plant out
T = Tree ⎭ permanently.
E = Evergreen
S-E = Semi-evergreen
D = Deciduous

Preparing your plan

Putting your ideas on paper If you intend to make only minor changes to an existing garden, and do the work yourself, a rough sketch and notes may well be enough. If you propose to lay out a completely new garden, or want to make major changes, then you need to go into more detail, especially if you are going to get some of the work done by contractors. Detailed drawings are vital to safeguard your own interests, not only to ensure you get the layout you intend, but also to enable the contractor to price the job properly, with no hidden extras. Without detailed drawings, unnecessary and sometimes costly quibbles and misunderstandings can arise.

Working drawings and specifications are normally necessary only where major building and construction work are involved. If such plans have to be approved by local councils, a good deal of information may be required. These plans are best left to the professionals to prepare.

Making a ground plan If you intend to carry out relatively small-scale im-

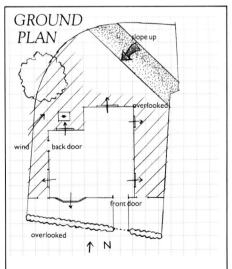

When finalizing your plan, include details of slopes, where the garden is overlooked and wind direction.

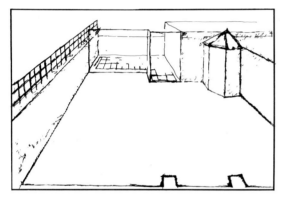

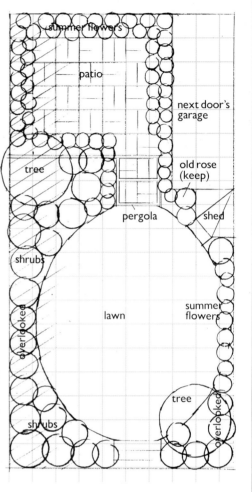

A GARDEN PLAN

A good way to plan your garden is to lay tracing paper over a photograph and sketch your design on it. Include the features you want to keep and think about how to disguise negative features. When your thoughts have been finalised, transfer all the details, to scale, to a graph-paper plan.

provements which do not affect the whole garden, then a simple sketch plan will probably suffice. In the case of a new flower bed or border, draw the outline of the area on to squared paper, which makes it easy to show the planting positions. Where a new building, or a feature like a rock garden or pool, is to be added to an existing layout, it is advisable to show the immediate surroundings on your plan. You will find it helpful to show reference points like paths, nearby buildings and boundaries. These are likely to affect access and siting.

For new layouts and major alterations, make a complete site assessment before you get down to drawing up your final plans and proposals. The following are some of the main points to look for:

★ *Ground form* Note the shape of the plot and measure it up. If you draw this to a convenient scale – say 3m (10ft) to 2.5cm (1in) – on squared paper, it will save time later when you come to plan the final layout. Mark clearly which direction is north. If the ground slopes appreciably, mark in the high and low spots to indicate the direction of any slopes.

★ *Walls, hedges and fences* Mark in existing boundaries, together with any internal divisions. Indicate which are walls, hedges and fences. At the same time, jot down ideas for improvements. Fences may need painting, replacing or removing; climbers can be planted against the wall; a new retaining wall or a new hedge can be put in. These notes will be helpful later on, when making final plans. Assess existing hedges. Are they tall enough to give privacy, reduce noise levels and dust entry from outside the garden? Do they provide sufficient

shelter from wind? Or are they too tall, blocking out light?

★ *Paths, drives and hard surfacing* Draw in all existing paths and hard-surfaced areas, indicating the type of surface: concrete, crazy paving, slabs or brick. Again, note if repairs or improvements are needed. Note, too, any paths that have been worn in lawns, where no 'formal' paths exist.

★ *Buildings and structures* Indicate the position and nature of existing buildings, including your greenhouse, shed and garage. Mark in entrances to the garden: doorways and French windows to the house.

★ *Other features* Mark in the location of rock gardens and pools. Show outstanding views, either within or outside the garden, and especially those seen from the windows of the house or from the patio. Eyesores should also be indica-

ted: manhole covers, drains, down spouts, bare or harsh walls within the garden and ugly views outside the garden.

★ *Lawns and planted areas* Show the shape, size and position of all lawns, beds and borders. Mark in any specimen shrubs or trees.

★ *Special growing conditions* Mark the shaded areas and any wet patches, as well as any particularly sheltered or exposed and windy spots

Drawing up the design Armed with your ground plan of existing features, prepare some sketch plans of your proposals. You can save time by placing a sheet of tracing paper over the prepared base plan and pencilling in your ideas. Prepare a separate tracing paper overlay for each alternative scheme. As you draw in the new features, include the measurements. Use photographs to help you visualise the finished scheme. Take several snaps from different positions in the garden: from the patio, the gate and windows. Again, you can draw your ideas on tracing paper overlays; this works well provided you work from a good-sized print and draw to scale.

Problems to avoid Double-check that your plans do fit within the area. Buildings, garage and greenhouse need to be behind the building line. If in doubt, check with your local authority that your scheme complies with planning and building regulations. If you don't want to fall out with your neighbours, consult them before putting up any high walling, fencing or buildings near common boundaries.

Make sure your final scheme is practical; not too ambitious; workable; easy to maintain; and not too costly, both in terms of implementation and future maintenance. Although hard surfaces are more costly to provide initially than lawns and planting, they need less aftercare.

If your garden is on a considerable slope, seriously consider terracing the steep banks and incorporating steps to make the going easier. In any event, avoid making lawns on slopes steeper than 1 in 3 because of mowing difficulties. Examine the possibility of planting with ground cover shrubs as an alternative. Greenhouses, children's play areas, drying lines and refuse bins all need to be within easy reach of the house, and all need suitable disguising. These and other practical considerations will be discussed in some detail in the following chapters.

Planting schemes It is a good ideal to plan and draw these on separate sheets, dealing with a single bed or border at a time and using squared paper. Before you finalise your list of suitable plants, you need to assess the site and soil conditions of your garden as previously indicated. As a general rule, simple schemes tend to be more successful than complicated ones. The character and shape of your garden is obviously going to be the major factor affecting the arrangement of planting detail.

Plants and shrubs can provide an excellent screen for features you would rather hide or minimise, such as a drain pipe (above) or shed (right). They can also serve as a perfect 'natural' frame (below) for doors or windows.

Preparing your work programme

It helps if the timing and order in which jobs are carried through follow a logical sequence. In practice this is not always feasible, perhaps due to personal circumstances, to weather and soil conditions, or to fitting in with the planting season.

There is usually plenty of scope for flexibility when implementing small scale improvements. You can choose fine weather to erect buildings and construct paths, and set out your plants when weather and soil conditions are just right. It is a different matter when it comes to new layouts and major improvements; timing is then of the utmost importance. It is easiest in the long run if you adopt a disciplined, systematic approach.

First you need to translate your paper plans into reality on the ground. Clear the site of unwanted rubbish and vegetation, then measure out and mark out, by hammering in short pegs, to show the precise positions of the various elements.

The following sequence is sound and works well in most situations. It is used as the basis for the order of the chapters that follow.

Step 1 Walls, fences and hedges Begin by providing the site boundaries – staking your claim, so to speak. Follow this up with any internal divisions, which provide the setting for the scheme.

The choice of climbers, their ground preparations and planting are also discussed briefly in this section, although the plants themselves are not set out until some time later.

Step 2 Paths, driveways and patios Next in priority is the selection and use of materials for hard surface areas. Paths and drives not only ensure ease of access while the rest of the work is under-

FIRST

PREPARING A FLOWER BED

Once the perimeters of your garden are established (1), you can begin to 'sculpt' and give it character. To define a flower bed, use your garden hose (2) until you have a satisfactory shape. Leaving the hose in place (3), dig out your bed to a depth of about a spit (4). Be sure to maintain a clear, crisp edge. Position your plants, still in their containers (5), until the arrangement suits you. Plant each firmly in place, remembering to water in, and your garden is on its way to the well-established mature look (6) that is the ideal.

4

taken, but also set the ground levels for lawns and planted areas. Make planting pockets in paved areas during the construction process.

The associated planting includes the selection and filling of containers, as well as the use of paving plants.

Step 3 Building and garden features Any excavations for buildings, pools and rock gardens are best carried out before making lawns. Provide and position children's sand pits, barbecue areas and compost corners.

The associated planting of pools and rock gardens can follow on at a more leisurely pace. Statuary, bird baths, garden furniture and play equipment as well as any lighting you wish to use can all be added later.

Step 4 Beds and borders – groundwork Draining and levelling, along with manuring, liming and ground preparations of necessity precede planting.

Step 5 Choosing plants Select, obtain and plant trees, shrubs and perennials. These take longer to mature and are often planted before lawns are laid.

Step 6 Lawns Prepare the ground and lay turves or seed lawn areas. Where there are young children in the family, lawn making takes priority over tree and shrub planting. Lawn plant alternatives should be considered at this stage.

Step 7 Fruit and vegetables Sow and plant crops in beds and borders; in containers; or intercropped among flowers. As food crops tend to contribute less to the appearance of a garden than shrubs and flowers, they tend to be left until last in the process of garden planning.

Step 8 Problems Deal with these if and when they should arise.

Work out an overall maintenance plan and programme.

Chapter 2

WALLS, FENCES AND HEDGES

Once walls and fences are erected, and hedges planted, they should last for many years – with little scope for change. And provided they are chosen wisely and well-maintained, they add greatly to the appearance and value of the home – and comfort of the garden.

In this chapter, the flexibility and adaptability of walls, fences and hedges are discussed, and the range of walling and fencing materials is reviewed in some detail. A selection of hedging has also been made; planting tips and guidelines for year-round care and training are given. In addition, the problem of dealing with hard, vertical surfaces is dealt with and there are lists of wall plants and climbers, which not only disguise or soften a bare wall or fence, but also add colour and texture to the garden.

The role of the vertical dimension

Walls, fences and hedges play an important role in the layout of most gardens, both functionally and aesthetically. It is wise to create a clear vertical demarcation of boundaries, and useful to divide one part of the garden from another. In the high density housing of today, there is often a need for privacy. Walls, fences and hedges provide screening and a means of shutting out eyesores.

Shelter and protection from the elements, and chilling winds in particular, are essential if gardens are to be enjoyed to the full, and plants given a chance. A vertical barrier between your garden and a busy thoroughfare can help keep down the levels of noise, dust and fumes, while at the same time keeping children and pets safely inside. For comfort, shade from strong sun is occasionally called for, but in our uncertain climate, it is better not to overdo the provision of shade.

Retaining walls prevent soil erosion and make terracing practical. And, to add interest to a flat site, they make sunken gardens and raised beds possible. Functional walls, hedges and fences also have an aesthetic presence and can provide attractive backdrops to planting, while climbers and wall plants can add further interest and beauty.

Points to consider When deciding whether to choose a wall, fence or hedge, compare their relative strong and weak points.

★ *Cost* Walls in general are the most costly, but good-quality permanent fencing is not far behind. Hedging requires the least outlay.

★ *Skill and ease of handling* Building a wall, especially if more than a few brick courses high, requires considerable time, effort and expertise, and should not be lightly undertaken. Fencing is relatively straightforward, and within

the capabilities of the average DIY enthusiast. Hedging is equally straight-forward, given a sensible choice of plants and a bit of attention to ground preparations, planting and aftercare.

★ *Appearance* Newly built walls, unless kept low, tend to dominate, often giving a hard, severe effect. Natural timber fencing blends into the garden less obtrusively. Living screens of hedging fit in best of all.

★ *Suitability* Walling can be used for curved and straight runs, and provides good support for climbers. Fencing gives instant results, but is best reserved for straight runs. Some make good plant supports. Hedging, excellent for straight and curved runs, may take a number of years to reach an effective height.

★ *Durability and maintenance* Walling can last a lifetime with little maintenance. Expect good fencing to provide up to about 25 years' service; cheaper kinds need replacing after a few years. All wooden fencing needs regular treatment to prevent rot. Hedging, although considered relatively permanent, is not immune to pests and diseases. Most hedging needs regular pruning or clipping.

★ *Soil effects* Walling has a drying effect on soil at its base; space plants at least 20cm (8in) away. Fencing doesn't exert much influence on the soil, unlike some hedging. Privet, for instance, has invasive roots which rob surrounding soil of food and moisture, so plants must be fed more generously than otherwise.

Walling

Materials Traditional walling is usually of brick, less often of stone. Brick is usually less expensive and more readily obtainable; stone requires a higher degree of skill when it comes to construction. Hewn stone is tricky to lay and cut, but dry-stone walling with its random-sized flints and rocks is even thicker. Brick is obtainable in various

colours, ranging from red, terracotta and rusty brown, to honey and purple. Always specify exterior quality, frost-proof brick; some bricks are totally unsuitable for outdoor use. (For bricks to be used below ground level, use a foundation brick, which is less than half the cost of a good facing brick.) Cotswold stone is honey-coloured; York sandstone yellowish brown; and limestone comes in shades of brown and grey.

Simulated stone is a cheaper man-made material, composed of rock dust and cement, and cast in convenient-sized blocks which are laid rather like bricks. Readily available, simulated stone comes in shades of pale green, brown, buff-grey and red. Concrete blocks, coloured or plain, provide even cheaper walling, and they are not difficult to lay. Screen blocks come in concrete or simulated stone. These blocks are pierced in various designs to allow light and air to filter through, and are excellent for walling around the patio to give privacy without cutting out too much light.

Types of walls

Walling is popularly used in a variety of ways.

Low walling makes an effective divider without obliterating the view and robbing light, but will do nothing to deter children, dogs and cats from straying. However, low walling will keep cars and bicycles out of your garden. Low walling can be constructed half-brick thickness, and made any height up to about 75cm (2½ft).

There are many ways to create boundaries which are attractive as well as effective. The choice of materials includes wood, brick and concrete, and height is a variable factor. Man-made fencing can be handsome on its own or can form an excellent backdrop for plants and shrubs.

This attractive cavity wall physically separates the terrace from the garden, yet unites them visually.

Cavity walling makes an attractive planter. Construct two walls of similar thickness and height, with a space between to take potting compost and plants.

Fencing

Wood must certainly be the most widely used of all fencing materials, and one of the most attractive. Natural timber blends in well and when maintained properly looks very smart. Regular treatment with preservative is needed to prevent rot. Good-quality timbers include long-lasting softwoods like cedar and larch, and hardwoods like oak and chestnut. Timber is used both for panelling and main supports.

Metal is used extensively through a whole range of products, from inexpensive netting and chain link to superior wrought-iron work. Metal needs protection from corrosion, especially near the sea, in towns, and along regularly gritted roads. Galvanising and plastic coating reduce maintenance; painted metal needs routine painting. Metal supports rank among the strongest and most durable.

Plastics are used both for panelling and supports, are easy to erect and require minimal maintenance. On the other hand, unless plastic fencing is reinforced with metal, it is among the least vandal-proof types of fencing.

Concrete is mainly reserved for inconspicuous positions. Posts and panelling are large, heavy and rather plain. When reinforced, concrete is strong and durable, needing virtually no maintenance, but concrete fencing is not particularly easy to put up single-handed. All concrete is fairly costly. Wood, metal and plastic fencing are available at low and high prices; the cost is geared to quality and durability.

Medium-to-high walling, kept below eye level, provides a good physical division and a certain degree of privacy and shelter, while still allowing you to retain visual contact with the outside. Walling above eye level is reserved primarily for screening and shelter, and is often built of pierced blocks. Be wary of building a high solid wall in exposed gardens; wind turbulence can become a problem. Walls up to eye-level height can be of half-brick thickness, provided they are well reinforced with piers.

Though more expensive, a whole brick thick makes a stronger job, and is nicer looking.

Retaining walls of 15cm (6in) make useful raised beds and small terraces. In theory, they can be constructed up to a height of 2m (7ft), but for appearance's sake and to avoid major construction problems, it is wise not to exceed a height of 1m (3½ft). It is far better to have two retaining walls of 1m (3½ft) than have a 2m (7ft) wall.

Types of fencing

Like walling, fencing can be used in a variety of ways.

Low dividers are useful where a minimal physical barrier will suffice: next to paths and driveways, for example.

★ *Post and chain* White plastic or painted timber posts, linked by lengths of single chain, usually plastic these days, can look distinctive in the right setting.

★ *Trip rail* Low plastic or painted timber rail, secured to timber or plastic posts, serves the same purpose.

★ *Bow top/regency* This continuous fencing in green plastic-coated wire is intended to be used as an edging for flower beds and paths.

Medium and high wire-type fencing can provide more security at a relatively low cost.

★ *Post and wire fencing* consists of two or three horizontal strands of galvanised or plastic-coated wire and is one of the cheapest forms of fencing. It is most effective when used with hedging.

★ *Wire mesh, and chain link fencing* are relatively inexpensive and easy to erect. They are sold by the roll and available galvanised and plastic coated. Wire mesh and chain-link fencing are functional, not beautiful, but can be used to support climbers. Much the same can be said of plastic mesh supports fixed to walls.

★ *Chestnut paling* is made of split chestnut pales wired together. Sold by the roll, it gives useful protection to young hedges.

Panel-type fencing ranks among the most attractive, long lasting and most expensive of fencing.

★ *Close-boarded,* treated, natural sawn timber panels, in 1.8m (6ft) lengths and heights up to 1.8m (6ft), are widely used. Whether of vertical or horizontal lapped board, or broad woven board,

they provide effective screening and shelter. Being close-boarded and solid, they catch the wind, and need very strong supports.

★ *Wattle fencing* is also made of wood and sold in panels, but is a bit less expensive and not quite as durable as close-boarded fencing.

★ *Concrete fencing* for ease of handling is normally obtainable in sections to make up 1.8 or 2m (6 or 7ft) panels.

★ *Fibreglass and plastic* panels, coloured or clear, tend to be expensive, and at present are used mainly for balcony and roof gardens.

Open style fencing can be very attractive on its own, or as a support for climbers and wall plants.

★ *Wrought-iron work and metal railings* can be ornate and expensive but they are usually strong and long lasting.

★ *Trellis work* in painted or natural treated timber provides effective screening. It is also available in white or

An open rail fence (below left) *creates a boundary; chain link fencing* (below) *allows the house to be viewed; and close-boarded fencing* (bottom) *ensures complete privacy.*

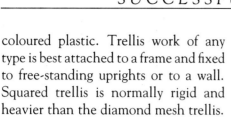
coloured plastic. Trellis work of any type is best attached to a frame and fixed to free-standing uprights or to a wall. Squared trellis is normally rigid and heavier than the diamond mesh trellis. Diamond trellis can be expanded or contracted to fit the frame.

★ *Post and rail fencing,* in sawn painted timber or rustic finish, is very versatile. Horizontal rails can be fixed as close or as wide apart as wished.

Fencing supports

Any fence is only as strong as its supports. Go for the best you can afford for permanent work.

Materials Treated sawn or debarked wood is usually 7.5 or 10cm (3 or 4in) square, either pointed to hammer home direct, or cut square to fit into metal post support sockets. Check the ends have been dipped in preservative before fixing. Tubular metal and angle iron posts provide excellent support. As with the fencing material, any ferrous metal posts need rust-proofing by galvanising, plastic coating or by painting with bitumen.

Concrete posts are rot proof and maintenance free. They are best set in concrete. High impact rigid plastic, along with other new materials, is finding its way on to the market. Maintenance is low and it is rot proof, but the material has yet to prove itself in the long term.

Length and spacing of supports To ensure proper anchorage, there needs to be an adequate length of post below ground as well as above. For 1.2m (4ft) high fencing allow for 60cm (2ft) below ground. For 1.8-2.4m (6-8ft) high fencing, allow 75cm (2½ft) below ground, but follow any manufacturer's recommendations.

As a rule-of-thumb guide, supports should not be spaced more than 2.7m (9ft) apart for netting; or 1.8-2m (6-7ft) for panel and open type fencing.

Growing climbers and wall plants

For practical purposes, there are two broad groups of climbers. The first includes the true climbing plants like ivy, clematis and Virginia creeper which need supports but are equipped with natural means of attachment. Ivy has aerial roots, clematis has twining stems and tendrils, and Virginia creeper produces sucker pads. Second are the wall plants. These are mostly shrubs, mainly self-supporting with strong stems and branches, and amenable to being trained against a wall or fence. True climbers are especially suitable for training over trellis work, rafters and pergolas, because true climbers are quicker growing with longer, more pliant, supple stems than wall plants.

Perennial and woody climbers and wall plants, once established, will continue to grow and flourish year after year. Annual climbers are discarded after flowering and need to be started each year from seed. Their chief value lies in their ability to give quick colour and screening.

Supports for climbers

Climbers have an important decorative and screening role to play, but they are not seen to best advantage unless properly supported.

Providing support

Ideally, all supports should be in position before planting. This not only ensures that support is to hand from the start but also avoids damage to plants.

The shade-tolerant camellia Donation (below) *does well against a north-facing wall; Virginia creeper* (below right) *needs fertile well-drained but moisture-retentive soil; pyracantha (firethorn) in berry adds colour to the side of a house* (below far right).

during erection. Methods of support vary considerably. There are various masonry nails with pieces of lead or plastic attached. These loop neatly round single stems and effectively hold them in. Look for the newer plastic plant ties with epoxy resin fixings which stick to brick or woodwork.

Wire Using lengths of galvanised or plastic-coated wire, threaded through eyelet hooks and fixed securely at each end, is a well tried method of supporting wall plants and climbers. Drill and plug the wall at not more than 1.2m (4ft) intervals in vertical and horizontal rows, and screw the eyelets into the wall. 14-gauge wire is usually enough.

Trellis This is a popular and traditional method of supporting wall plants. Often trellis panels are nailed directly on to a wall; but it is infinitely better to screw trellis on to a light timber frame of 5×2.5cm (2×1in) battens. (Be sure to treat all woodwork with preservative.) The batten frame is fixed to the wall either by keyhole eyes and hooks or by screws, after first drilling and plugging the wall. Fixing trellis work to a frame creates a space between the wall and trellis. This minimises the risk of damage by ivy, climbing hydrangea and Virginia creeper, all of which can damage crumbling brickwork or masonry. It also allows free air circulation, cutting down the likelihood of damp pockets – healthier for plant and building alike. Be sure to use galvanised/rust-proofed screws and fixings.

Overhead rafters, pergolas and walkways

Vertical supports and rafters over patios and hard surfaced areas are becoming increasingly popular. A walkway of supports and overhead rafters can also be put up relatively simply, at reasonable cost, to provide an excellent support for climbers.

Erect two lines of pairs of 10×10cm (4×4in) treated timber posts; space them about 2m (7ft) apart each way (between posts and between rows). Use the metal socket spikes mentioned earlier and ensure the length of post allows 2m (7ft) headroom, preferably more. Use galvanised bolts to connect cross rails of 10×4cm (4×1½in) timbers to joint the tops of each pair of posts – as well as along each side. Then bolt or screw lighter cross rafters midway between each main rafter. Crisscross supporting wires as necessary. Plant climbers at the foot of each post and tie in at regular intervals.

Planting Climbers

1 Choose sturdy, healthy, well rooted plants suited to your garden, taking into account plant requirements and existing conditions.

2 Carry out planting at the correct time of year: September/October or March/April for evergreens, and autumn/early winter for deciduous plants. Container-grown plants can be set out almost any

Climbers and wall plants

Name	Ht×sp	Position	Soil	Nature/season of interest	Habit
A. *Abutilon megapotamicum* Flowering maple	2×1.5m (7×5ft)	○ ◑	N	Red and yellow flowers in summer	S-E Sh
B. *Berberidopsis corallina* Coral plant	4×3m (13×10ft)	◑ ●	A N	Red flowers in summer	E Cl
C. *Campsis grandiflora* Trumpet vine	6×4m (20×13ft)	○	A N C	Orange and red flowers in summer	D Cl
D. *Ceanothus* 'Autumnal Blue' California lilac	3.5×3m (12×10ft)	○	A N C	Blue flowers in summer and autumn	E Sh
E. *Chaenomeles speciosa* vars Flowering quince	1-3×1.5-3m (3½-10×5-10ft)	○ ◑ ●	A N C	Pink, red or white flowers in spring; yellow fruits in autumn	D Sh
F. *Chimonanthus praecox* vars Wintersweet	2.4×2m (8×7ft)	○	A N C	Yellow and purple scented flowers in winter and spring	D Sh
G. *Clematis* various Virgin's bower	3-9×2-6m (10-30×7-20ft)	○ ◑	N C	Red, pink, blue or white flowers from spring to autumn	D-E Cl
H. *Cotoneaster horizontalis* Fishbone cotoneaster	2×2.4m (7×8ft)	○ ◑ ●	A N C	Pinky white flowers in summer, red winter berries	D Sh
J. *Euonymus fortunei* vars Winter creeper	4.5×4.5m (15×15ft)	◑ ●	A N C	Green or variegated white/gold leaves	E Cl
K. *Forsythia suspensa* Weeping forsythia	2.4×3m (8×10ft)	○ ◑ ●	A N C	Yellow flowers in spring	D Sh
L. *Garrya elliptica* Silk tassel	4×3m (13×10ft)	◑ ●	A N C	Grey-green catkins in winter	E Sh
M. *Hedera* various ivy	6×6m (20×20ft)	○ ◑ ●	A N C	Green or variegated leaves	E Cl
N. *Hydrangea petiolaris* Climbing hydrangea	3.5×3m (12×10ft)	◑ ●	A N	White flowers in summer	D Cl

Clematis

Euonymus fortunei

Forsythia

Climbers and wall plants

Name	Ht×sp	Position	Soil	Nature/season of interest	Habit
O. *Jasminum nudiflorum* Winter-flowering jasmine	4×1.5m (13×5ft)	○ ◑	A N C	Yellow flowers from autumn to spring	D Sh
P. *Lonicera periclymenum* Honeysuckle	5×4m (17×13ft)	○ ◑	A N C	Yellow, white and purple scented flowers in summer	D Cl
Q. *Parthenocissus quinquefolia* Virginia creeper	7×6m (23×20ft)	○ ◑ ●	A N C	Red and crimson autumn leaves	D Cl
R. *Passiflora caerulea* Passion flower	6×3m (20×10ft)	○	A N C	White and purple flowers in summer followed by orange fruits	S-E Cl
S. *Polygonum baldschuanicum* Mile-a-minute	6×6m (20×20ft)	○ ◑	A N C	White flowers in summer	D Cl
T. *Pyracantha* various Firethorn	4-6×3m (13-20×10ft)	○ ◑ ●	A N C	White flowers in summer, red berries in autumn and winter	E Sh
W. *Rosa* various Rose	2.4-6×3m (8-20×10ft)	○ ◑	A N C	Orange, pink, red, yellow or white flowers in summer and autumn; red hips in autumn	D Cl
X. *Vitis coignetiae* Crimson glory vine	9×9m (30×30ft)	○ ◑	N	Orange and crimson autumn leaves; blue-black autumn fruits	D Cl
Y. *Wisteria* various Wisteria	6×12in (20×40ft)	○	A N	Mauve, violet or white scented flowers in summer	D Cl

Climbers and wall plants for special purposes:

Climbers for north and east aspects
B, E, H, J, K, L, M, N, O, P, Q, S, T

Climbers for south and west aspects
A, C, D, E, F, G, H, J, M, O, Q, R, S, T, W, X, Y

Quick-growing climbers
Suitable for pergolas, pillars and rafters
B, C, G, M, Q, S, X, Y

Flowering climbers
A, B, C, D, E, F, G, H, K, L, N, O, P, R, S, T, W, X, Y

Evergreen climbers
B, D, J, L, M, T

Berrying and fruiting climbers
E, H, R, T, W, X

Climbers for cold sites
E, G, H, K, M, N, O, Q, S, T, W

Lonicera periclymenum

Vitis coignetiae

Wisteria

time, provided that the ground is not waterlogged or frozen, and that you are prepared to give them extra care and attention.

3 Dig a planting hole at least 45cm (18in) wide and 40cm (16in) deep, or twice as wide and half as deep again as the root ball, in the case of large container-grown climbers. The base of the stem should be set at least 20-30cm (8-12in) from the foot of the wall or other support. Fork over the bottom of the planting hole, working in a bucketful of peat or rotted compost, plus a handful of bonemeal. Add plenty of coarse sand as well if the soil is inclined to be heavy.

4 Water the plant thoroughly. If necessary, soak containers in a bucket of water until the air bubbles stop rising. Drain for approximately thirty minutes before planting.

5 Test the depth of the hole with the plant still in its container or rootball wrapping. Put sufficient good topsoil or potting compost into the bottom of the hole so that the plant will finally rest 2cm (¾in) deeper than before the move. Put in a cane, as temporary support is often needed to lead the stems to their permanent supports.

6 Remove the container or wrapping. Set the plant in position, spread out the roots, cutting back any which are damaged to sound tissue. Backfill with good, crumbly topsoil or potting compost like John Innes No 2. Firm the soil around the roots as filling proceeds.

7 Immediately after planting, shorten any damaged stems back to a healthy bud. Tie in the stems of plants needing support, and water in to settle the soil.

Pruning and training

Pruning is necessary to keep plants healthy and tidy, as well as to maintain a succession of new flowering and fruit-ing shoots. How climbers and wall plants are pruned and trained depends on the type of plant and the growing conditions.

With young plants, tie in new growths to prevent them flopping or blowing about. Space the stems out evenly to let in light and air and to display the plants to maximum effect. Free-standing, self-supporting wall plants are best encouraged to retain their natural shape.

Guidelines

Some fairly typical pruning methods:

1 Plants which bloom in spring on shoots produced the previous year are pruned in late spring, immediately after flowering. Cut out the old flowered shoots and tie in replacement ones. *Clematis montana* is a prime example. Rambler roses are treated in a broadly similar manner, but the flowered stems are cut out in summer.

Clematis montana 'Rubens', *ascending over wooden beams, forms a natural triumphal arch.*

2 Summer and autumn-blooming plants which flower on the tips of new growths are pruned either immediately after flowering or early spring. Aim to provide a main framework of branches and cut out old flowered side shoot back to this framework. Many of the large-flowered hybrid clematis and the climbing HT and modern roses fall into this category.

3 Flowering quince and many strong growing flowering wall plants and climbers bloom on older wood. Wisteria blooms on short spurs on older wood. Prune after flowering, cutting back new shoots to three or five leave (summer pruning). Shorten back the late summer growths of wisteria in February.

4 Slow-growing plants like winter sweet, which flower on two- or three year-old stems, are usually thinned ou

during or just after flowering. Remove the oldest, flowered shoots.

5 Foliage climbers like ivy and Virginia creeper are usually allowed to fill their allotted space, and are then clipped as necessary to keep them within bounds. This is usually best carried out in spring or early summer.

6 Slow-growing plants of neat habit like fishbone cotoneaster are left alone, except for occasional cutting to shape and thinning of overcrowded shoots.

Planting a hedge

Thorough preparation is necessary if a new hedge is to get off to a good start. Don't skimp; the hedge is likely to occupy the ground for many years to come.

1 Dig a 90cm (3ft) strip to a full spade's depth at least 14-21 days before planting, to allow the soil to settle. While you are digging, fork the bottom spit to break up compacted soil. Work in one or two bucketfuls of well rotted manure, garden compost or peat, plus a handful of bonemeal and a small handful of John Innes bases fertiliser per m (yd) run. On heavy soil, fork in plenty of sharp sand as well. If the ground is low lying and slow draining, ridge up the centre of the strip by about 30cm (12in).

2 Choose hedging plants to suit your garden. Set out evergreens in September/October or March/April. Bare-rooted deciduous hedging is best planted out in autumn/early winter. Both deciduous and evergreen container-grown hedging can, if necessary, be planted out at almost any time, provided you have time to give extra attention to watering and syringing during the summer months. Never work soil or plant if it is frozen or waterlogged.

3 Water all plants and allow to drain or half an hour before planting. Stand bare-rooted plants overnight in a bucket of water.

4 A single row of hedging will normally suffice; plant at the spacings indicated in the table. Use pegs and a taut garden line to indicate the centre of the strip. Set the plants at the same depth as before the move, firming the soil around the roots and watering in.

5 During the first dormant period after planting, cut back deciduous hedging plants by about half to make them bushy. Leave the tops of conifers uncut until they reach the required height.

6 In exposed gardens, protect newly planted hedges from wind, using either fine mesh netting screens or temporary fencing such as wattle. In the absence of walling or permanent fencing, on boundaries bordering footpaths and drives, put up temporary fencing, such as chestnut paling.

7 Apply a mulch of well rotted garden compost in spring, and repeat annually.

Aftercare

Keep young plants weed free and well watered for the first two or three years after planting, and syringe the foliage during warm or windy weather.

Clip young deciduous hedges frequently – two or three times between spring and late summer – shortening new growths by about a third each time. Evergreens tend to need less severe and less frequent cutting. Remember to leave the tops of conifers uncut until the desired height is reached. For large-leaved hedging like laurel, use secateurs. With shears or trimmers there is a risk of cutting leaves in half, with a subsequent browning at the leaf edges. Keep the top of your hedging narrower than the base, otherwise bare stems may result.

In the second and later years, give an annual spring feed of a small handful of John Innes base fertilizer per m (yd) run.

Pruning established hedges

Always prune at the correct time (see Hedging table on pages 30-31).

Formal deciduous hedging should be pruned regularly, after not more than 20-25cm (8-10in) of top growth is made. Shorten back the new shoots by a third to a half, two or three times a season if necessary. Prune the sides as well, keeping the top of the hedge narrower than the base. Regular pruning makes for a thick, dense hedge.

Informal hedging is often allowed to reach its final height without the top growth being pruned. The sides, however, need regular clipping. If branching is sparse and growth thin, prune back hard to encourage bushiness. You may lose a season's flowering, but the result will be a denser, more attractive hedge. Deadhead flowering hedges by clipping, unless berries or fruits are a feature.

Conifer hedging is normally left with the top growth unpruned until it has reached its required height. Formal evergreen hedging, such as holly, often has the growing point removed in the early stages. Both conifer and broad-leaved evergreen hedging benefit from regular clipping of side growth.

A row of conifers makes an effective and dramatically attractive hedge.

Hedging plants

Name	Ht	Spacing	Cut	Position	Features	Habit
A. *Berberis*						
1. *darwinii*	1.8m 6ft	60cm 2ft	Summer	○ ◑	Orange flowers and green leaves	E
2. *thunbergii* Barberry	1.8m 6ft	60cm 2ft	Winter	○	Yellow flowers and red leaves	D
B. *Buxus sempervirens* & vars Box	2m 7ft	40cm 16in	Spring/ Summer	○ ◑ ●	Green or yellow leaves	E
C. *Chamaecyparis lawsoniana* & vars Lawson Cypress	3m 10ft	90cm 3ft	Summer	○ ◑	Green, yellow or blue foliage	E
D. *Cotoneaster lacteus* Cotoneaster	3m 10ft	75cm 2½ft	Summer	○ ◑	White flowers and red berries	E
E. *Crataegus monogyna* Quickthorn	2.4m 8ft	30cm 12in	Summer	○	White flowers and red berries	D
F. *Cupressocyparis leylandii* & vars Leyland Cypress	4.5m 15ft	100cm 3½ft	Spring/ Summer	○ ◑	Green or yellow foliage	E
G. *Elaeagnus × ebbingei* & vars Elaeagnus	3m 10ft	90cm 3ft	Summer	○ ◑	Green, silvery or variegated leaves	E
H. *Escallonia* hybrids Escallonia	1.8m 6ft	75cm 2½ft	Spring/ Summer	○ ◑	Glossy green leaves and pink, red or white flowers	D
I. *Fagus sylvatica* & vars Beech	2.4m 8ft	45cm 18in	Summer	○ ◑	Green or purple leaves	D
J. *Fuchsia* 'Riccartonii' Fuchsia	1.8m 6ft	75cm 2½ft	Spring	○ ◑	Red and purple flowers	D
K. *Hebe anomala* Shrubby Veronica	1m 3½ft	45cm 18in	Summer	○	White flowers	E
L. *Ilex aquifolium* & vars Holly	2m 7ft	45cm 18in	Summer	○ ◑	Green or variegated leaves and red berries	E
M. *Lavandula spica* & vars Lavender	0.3-1.2m 1-4ft	30-40cm 12-16in	Summer/ Spring	○	Blue flowers and grey leaves	E
N. *Ligustrum ovalifolium* & vars Privet	2m 7ft	40cm 16in	Spring/ Autumn	○ ◑	Green or variegated leaves	S-E

Chamaecyparis lawsoniana

Crataegus monogyna

Escallonia

Name	Ht	Spacing	Cut	Position	Features	Habit
O. *Lonicera nitida* & vars Shiny Honeysuckle	1.8m 6ft	30cm 12in	Spring/ Summer	○ ◑	Green or yellow leaves	E
P. *Potentilla fruticosa* & vars Shrubby cinquefoil	1.2m 4ft	60cm 2ft	Spring/ Summer	○	White, yellow, flame or red flowers	D
Q. *Prunus* 1. ×*cistena* 'Crimson Dwarf' Purple-leaved sand cherry	1.2m 4ft	75cm 2½ft	Summer	○	White flowers and purple-red foliage	D
2. *laurocerasus* & vars Laurel	2m 7ft	90cm 3ft	Summer	◑ ●	Green leaves and red berries	E
R. *Pyracantha rogersiana* & vars Firethorn	2m 7ft	50cm 20in	Spring/ Summer	○ ◑	White flowers and red berries	E
S. *Ribes sanguineum* & vars Flowering currant	1-2.4m 3½-8ft	75cm 2½ft	Autumn	○ ◑ ●	Pink or red flowers	D
T. *Rosmarinus* 'Miss Jessop's Variety' Rosemary	1.8m 6ft	50cm 20in	Spring	○	Blue flowers and grey-green leaves	E
U. *Rosa* 'Kathleen Harrop' Rose	1.5m 5ft	90cm 3ft	Autumn/ Spring	○ ◑	Pink flowers	D
V. *Symphoricarpos* 'White Hedger' Snowberry	1.5m 5ft	90cm 3ft	Spring	○	White berries	D
W. *Tamarix gallica* Tamarisk	1.5m 5ft	60cm 2ft	Spring	○	Pink flowers	D
X. *Taxus baccata* & vars Yew	1.8m 6ft	60cm 2ft	Summer	○ ◑	Green or variegated foliage and red berries	E
Y. *Thuja occidentalis* Arbor Vitae	3m 10ft	60cm 2ft	Summer	○ ◑	Green or gold foliage	E
Z. *Viburnum tinus* & vars Laurustinus	2.4m 8ft	60cm 12in	Spring	○	White flowers and red berries	E

Note: The hedging plants listed can be grown in reasonable garden soils ranging from slightly acid to chalky

Hedging for special purposes:

Flowering hedges
A, D, E, H, J, K, M, P, Q1, R, S, T, U, W, Z

Berrying and fruiting hedges
A, D, E, L, Q2, R, U, V, X, Z

Evergreen hedges
A1, B, C, D, F, G, K, L, M, O, Q2, R, T, X, Y, Z

Hedges for cold sites
A, C, E, I, L, N, R, S, V, X

Boundary hedges
A, C, D, E, F, G, I, L, N, Q2, X, Y

Taxus baccata

Ribes sanguineum

Symphoricarpos 'White Hedger'

Chapter 3

PATHS, PATIOS AND DRIVES

However congenial to the eye, and pleasant underfoot, a velvety green sward has limitations – notably when it comes to taking the punishment of hard wear and use in all weathers. This is where it is wise to turn to hard surfacing. In this chapter, we discuss the most popular types, together with guidelines for proper laying and subsequent aftercare.

The patio, an old idea borrowed from warmer climes and adapted over the years, is today commonplace. And virtually indispensable to any respectable patio comes an assortment of containers and plants – to provide colour, fragrance and interest, if not throughout the year, certainly during the warmer months. So we have included details of window boxes, hanging baskets, tubs and planters, together with points to watch for when making your choice.

Planning hard surfaces

Before you lay any new hard surfacing, plan carefully, especially the routes of paths. Direct from door to destination is best, otherwise visitors are likely to take short cuts across your lawn or flower beds. Unless there is a very good reason, avoid sharp bends, and resist the temptation for undue fussiness. Straight-edged or gently curving paths and drives, bordering lawns, make for easier mowing and edging, without necessarily spoiling the look of the layout.

Make paths and drives wide enough for comfort: about 90cm (3ft) minimum for paths and 2.7m (9ft) for driveways. If you intend to take outdoor living seriously, you will need at least 3-4 sq m (sq yd) of patio per person, to allow for furniture, planting and walking space.

Choosing materials

Hard surfacing materials vary considerably one from another, and not all are suitable for the same purpose. Look around garden centres, DIY stores, and builders' merchants to see what is available locally. Get details and make sure that prices quoted include delivery to your door. Hard-surfacing materials are heavy and carriage from afar can prove expensive.

Consider the various surfacing materials from several angles. In addition to availability and price, the chosen material should look good and blend in well with your house and garden. Weigh up the possibility of glare from shiny or very light-coloured surfaces. Don't overlook the safety factor; make non-slip, non-trip, easy-to-walk-on materials a priority.

Go for practical surfaces that will stand up to wear and tear – punishing on drives. Obtain exterior grade materials; these are less likely to break up with constant wetting and drying, freezing and baking. Bear in mind, too,

The warm clay texture of this path leads eye and foot gently to the conservatory.

the degree of maintenance. And if you are doing a DIY job, go for easy-to-handle and lay materials – small-size paving slabs score here. There are three basic types of surface finish, in terms of texture, from which to choose.

The fine-textured finish is very practical for patios and heavily used paths and drives. Constructed from large, smooth, paving slabs or poured in-situ concrete, it provides a firm, even surface that is comfortable and safe to walk on, and easy to sweep and hose.

Rough-textured finish These are more decorative than functional and are best reserved for less frequently used but conspicuous areas, or where walking is not to be encouraged! Granite setts and

cobbles, whether real or artificial, can look highly attractive. They are not as easy to walk on, or as safe, as the fine finish, and they are more difficult to keep clean, as soil and dirt tend to lodge. Bricks are a special case in that they are fairly rough in texture but form a good surface for paths and patios. They are expensive but, for many people, they are the most attractive surfacing material of all.

Loose and soft binding surfaces Gravel and chippings can make a serviceable driveway if laid on very substantial foundations, but it is better to view these materials, along with bark, as a temporary measure or for little used paths. Asphalt and macadam, expertly laid and well maintained, make reasonable paths and driveways, but if badly laid and poorly maintained they break up disappointingly early.

Summary of hard surfacing materials

Material	Cost	DIY	Maintenance	Looks	Life
Asphalt	Medium	Average	Moderate	Plain/moderately attractive	Average
Bark	Medium/low	Quick	High/moderate	Moderately attractive	Short
Brick	High	Slow	Moderate/low	Attractive/ distinctive	Long
Cobble, in mortar	Medium	Slow	Moderate	Attractive	Long
Cobble, loose	Medium/low	Quick	Moderate/high	Attractive	Average
Concrete, poured	Medium	Average	Low	Plain	Long
Crazy paving	Medium/low	Slow	Low/moderate	Attractive	Average
Gravel, loose	Medium/low	Quick	High/moderate	Moderately attractive	Short
Gravel, rolled	Medium/low	Moderate/quick	High/moderate	Plain	Average/short
Macadam	Medium	Average	Moderate	Plain/moderately attractive	Average
Paving					
Pre-cast concrete	Medium/low	Moderate/quick	Low	Plain	Average/long
Reconstructed stone	Medium/high	and	Low	Moderately attractive	Long
Natural stone	High	fairly easy	Low	Distinctive	Long
Setts					
Concrete blocks	Medium/high	Moderate/slow	Moderate	Attractive	Long
Granite	High	Slow	Moderate	Attractive	Long
Timber	Medium/high	Average	High	Attractive	Average

Slate set in to concrete gives a durable patterned patio surface.

Paving and surfacing materials

Paving slabs Slabs of paving are among the most popular materials for the DIY enthusiast. They are quicker and generally easier to lay than bricks or setts. Traditionally square or rectangular, they range in size from about 30cm (12in) square to 90×60cm (3×2ft) and vary in thickness from 4-5cm (1½-2in). Modern concrete paving includes hexagonal and circular slabs to make interesting variations, but they work out more costly.

★ *Natural stone*, like York sandstone, in mellow sandy shades, looks good but is very costly to buy.

★ *Reconstructed stone*, a man-made alternative, is cheaper and a reasonable look-alike.

★ *Concrete slabs* are the least expensive, and are available in grey, buff, red, honey, charcoal, green or brown.

Bricks, setts and crazy paving These materials lend themselves to highly decorative treatment, either used alone or in conjunction with paving slabs.

★ *Bricks* vary in hardness and ability to withstand frost, so be sure to buy outdoor grades which are sold as paviors or walling bricks, with a good appearance on the 'bed face', and are frost proof. Bricks are available in pinks, reds, honey, blue-purple and terra-cotta. They are slow to lay and are often condemned as the surface becomes uneven and perhaps even dangerous. However, the fault is usually traced to inferior foundations causing

uneven settlement. Similar problems can arise with setts, crazy paving and stepping stones.

★ *Granite setts* are usually 10cm (4in) cubes, but 10×10×20cm (4×4×8in) setts are also available. Setts provide the hardest wearing surface, but are prohibitively expensive.

★ *Pre-cast concrete setts* are relatively cheap but also less hard wearing.

★ *Crazy paving*, made of pieces of broken paving, can provide a pleasing surface, especially if colours and sizes are tastefully varied. Crazy paving has a bad reputation for breaking up, but this is usually the result of shoddy workmanship when laying and not the fault of the materials.

★ *Concrete paving blocks* in interlocking patterned shapes or of simple, brick-sized proportions, lend themselves to brick-type treatment. Unlike bricks, they are designed to fit close to each other, without mortar joints between. They are proprietary products and the manufacturers issue laying instructions.

★ *Screen-pierced blocks* make a reasonably hard-wearing surface when laid flat, filled with soil and seeded with grass, and special blocks are now made, capable of carrying vehicular loads.

Gravel and bitumen surfaces

★ *Loose surfaces of aggregate*, such as limestone chippings, provide a quick, easy-to-lay path or drive. However, loose aggregate surfaces can be difficult to walk on; tend to collect dirt and become mixed with soil; and end up on lawns, with subsequent risk to mower blades. These surfaces need raking, weeding and topping up if they are to remain attractive. Rolled gravel over a hard base can overcome some of these problems, but is still not entirely satisfactory. Hoggin is a suitable path gravel with a clay content, which allows it to be rolled to a compact surface.

★ *Loose cobblestones* laid on a weed-free base can be decorative and nearly as effective as water to provide a 'no-go' area.

There is an enormous range of paving materials and the effects you can create: brick paviors (below left) match the colour and texture of the walls; brick line and concrete slabs set into cobblestones (below) give a variegated surface; a rough brick path blends in to the setting of a country cottage (below bottom); wooden slabs (right) are natural, yet exotic; while the mix of brick, concrete and paving stone seems perfect for a formal garden (far right).

★ *Asphalt and tarmacadam* These are both forms of top coating, usually in black, less often in red or green. Asphalt is more expensive, less able to stand any ground movement, and is really only suitable if there is a need to waterproof the base. Asphalt and tarmacadam drives break badly at the edge unless they have a curb or the foundation extends out under the adjoining turf. These materials, and related proprietary materials, are best laid by professionals, but some types can be laid cold by the DIY enthusiast. Consult your builders' merchant if in doubt.

Concrete Concrete laid in-situ over a hardcore base provides a durable and functional surface for path or drive.

Timber and bark fibre Timber board, usually seen as a raised platform near ground level or as roof-garden decking, is popular in hot countries. When well maintained, it looks pleasing, but with modern, crop-grown timber, it is essential to use pressure-impregnated wood to avoid rot. A drawback of timber surfacing is that, when wet, it can be slippery and slimy. Timber logs, set vertically in the ground, on a firm base and packed with bark fibre, make an

effective landscape path. Bark fibre on its own suffers the same shortcomings as loose aggregate.

Edging and paving plants

You can relieve the harsh appearance that hard surfacing sometimes has by setting out edging and paving plants. The first step is to select plants which are suitable for this purpose.

Planting perennial edging and paving plants

When making a patio, leave out the odd slab or two. When laying paving, cut off the odd corner or two, leaving planting pockets. Where paving is already laid, prise up some slabs to make a space for planting.

To prepare planting holes, scrape out any old soil, sand and hardcore. Make up a planting compost of two parts good topsoil to one part each of peat and sharp sand. Mix in a handful of John Innes Base fertiliser per bucketful of compost. Alternatively use John Innes No 2 potting compost. Fill up large pockets.

Normally it is best to use pot-grown plants and set them out in autumn or spring. Water the plants thoroughly, and allow to drain for 30 minutes before removing them from their pots. Check the roots for pieces of small crock and remove any you find. Dig out planting holes with a trowel, fill in around the rootball with moist potting compost or planting mix, firming in with your fingers. Finish off with the top of the rootball about 1cm (½in) below the surface. Where plants are set in crevices in paving, top with a 1cm (½in) of chippings. This covering helps plants in many ways; it keeps roots cool, retains moisture, discourages weeds and slugs, as well as preventing surface compaction and soil being washed away.

Patio containers

Buying containers Patio containers come in a bewildering array of sizes, shapes and materials. There are several points to consider before making your purchase.

★ *Size* Don't skimp, or the compost will dry out too quickly and hold inadequate food reserves. Window-boxes need to be at least 18cm (7in) wide and deep.

Hardy perennial edging and paving plants

Name	Ht × sp	Position	Nature/season of interest	Habit	
A. *Acaena microphylla* New Zealand burr	5×20cm 2×8in	○ ◑	Crimson burr-like fruits in late summer	Carpeter	E
B. *Armeria maritima* Thrift	10×20cm 4×8in	○ ◑	Pink, red or white flowers in summer	Tufty mound former	E
C. *Campanula garganica* Bellflower	10×30cm 4×12in	○	Blue flowers in summer	Tufty and spreading	E
D. *Dianthus* various Rock pinks	8-30×30cm 3-12×12in	○	Red, pink or white flowers in summer	Tufted or clump former	E
E. *Erigeron karvinskianus* Fleabane	25×45cm 10×18in	○	Pink, red or white flowers in summer	Spreading	E
F. *Erinus alpinus* Fairy foxglove	10×15cm 4×6in	○ ◑	Carmine, purple or white flowers in spring and summer	Tufted and compact	E
G. *Festuca ovina* 'Glauca' Fescue	15×15cm 6×6in	○	Blue-green grassy foliage spring to autumn	Tufty clumps	E
H. *Gysophila repens* 'Rosea' Baby's breath	15×40cm 6×16in	○	Rose-pink flowers in summer	Prostrate	D
I. *Hypericum empetrifolium* St John's wort	5×20cm 2×8in	○	Orange-yellow flowers in summer	Mat former	E
J. *Mentha requienii* Creeping mint	3×25cm 1×10in	◑ ●	Violet flowers in summer and aromatic foliage	Creeper	D
K. *Phlox douglasii* Alpine phlox	8×25cm 3×10in	○	Mauve, pink or white summer flowers	Mat former	E
L. *Saxifraga* (mossy) vars Saxifrage	3-8×25cm 1-3×10in	◑	Pink, red, yellow or white flowers in spring	Mat former	E
M. *Sedum spurium* Stonecrop	10×30cm 4×12in	○	Pink and red flowers in summer	Spreading	E
N. *Silene schafta* Campion/Catchfly	10×20cm 4×8in	○	Rose-red flowers in late summer/autumn	Carpeter	E
O. *Thymus serpyllum* Thyme	3-5×30cm 1-2×12in	○	Red, pink and white flowers in summer and aromatic foliage	Creeping	E
P. *Veronica prostrata* Speedwell	3-10×40cm 1-4×16in	○	Blue flowers in summer	Creeping	E

Note: All plants listed do best in neutral or chalky conditions

Edging and paving plants for special purposes:

Plants for edging
B, C, D, E, F, G, H, I, K, L, M, N, O, P

Plants for paving
A, B, D, F, H, I, J, K, L, N, O, P

Erinus alpinus

Festuca ovina 'Glauca'

Saxifraga (mossy)

Permanent shrubs and trees need a 30-35cm (12-14in) diameter container, or even larger.

★ *Drainage* Good drainage is essential. Check that there are enough drainage holes in the bottom of the container to prevent waterlogging.

★ *Appearance* The container needs to be of pleasing design, and appropriate for the intended setting. It should be stable and not liable to blow over.

★ *Weather resistance* Containers intended for year-round use need to be capable of standing up to the odd knock, and to frost. Some terracotta pots, especially imported ones, can split and shatter in frozen conditions.

★ *Insulation* Plant roots need protection from extremes of temperature, and good insulation will help plants survive harsh conditions. Timber tubs are among the best.

★ *Durability and cost* Consider the probable life span of a container in relation to its cost.

★ *Maintenance* This can be high; timber, for example, needs regular treatment.

Container materials

Again, the choice is dependent on your own taste, budget, availability, and the amount of maintenance you are prepared to do.

★ *Wood* This is attractive, a good insulator and easy to use, DIY fashion. On the other hand, wood is liable to rot and needs regular treatment with preservative. It is fairly long lasting if treated. Wood is inclined to be heavy.

★ *Wood fibre* A short-life moulded lightweight material, wood fibre is used to make liners for hanging baskets and as small-to-medium-sized containers in its own right.

★ *Plastics* These rust- and rot-proof materials are lightweight and practical. Heavy grade (including fibreglass)

Containers come in a variety of shapes, from pots and old sinks to this attractive painted wooden wheelbarrow.

planters, tubs, troughs, pots, window-boxes and hanging baskets may last for years. Flexible thin grades, however, have a short life. All need added insulation in winter.

★ *Terracotta, clay and ceramics* These look highly attractive, but some are liable to burst if the contents become frozen.

★ *Metal* Tubs and planters are occasionally made of metal, and are best used with an inner container. Old-fashioned ones of iron or lead are heavy and expensive. Aluminium alloy is light but tends to lose paint quickly. Metal containers need painting inside with rubberised bitumen, or there is a possible risk to plants; ferrous metals need painting regularly in order to prevent rust.

★ *Wire and plastic mesh* These are

excellent for traditional hanging baskets, but check that the wire is galvanised or plastic coated.

★ *Concrete* Containers made of concrete are rust and rot proof but heavy, and some are inclined to be very basic looking. It is a good material for making sink gardens.

★ *Stone* This is similar to concrete in terms of weight. Real stone looks good but is very costly.

Container type and use Containers are designed to meet fairly specific situations. Think carefully about your garden, and what you aim to achieve, before settling for any container.

★ *Windowboxes and wall planters* are invaluable for brightening up an expanse of wall, providing 'vertical' colour. Spring and summer bedding plants are those most often used.

★ *Hanging baskets* also provide interest at a height. They are normally viewed from all sides and below, hence their circular shape and use of trailing plants. Hanging baskets are fully exposed to the elements, so their use is almost exclusively confined to sheltered spots, the warmer months and summer bedding.

★ *Shrub and tree tubs* are normally large, square or round, and take considerable quantities of compost to sustain specimen plants. Attractive tubs, with tall narrow conifers or clipped topiary, look impressive set in pairs to flank a doorway or entrance. Try them in corners, too, to offset the drab squareness of a patio.

★ *Sinks and troughs* are becoming increasingly popular for the creation of gardens in miniature. When planted with a dwarf conifer or two, plus a few colourful rock and alpine plants, a sink garden is a source of lasting interest. It must have a minimum depth of 10-15cm (4-6in). Sinks are seen to best advantage if raised on firm blocks to bring them closer to eye level. (Raising them off the ground also improves drainage.) These containers can be purpose made from concrete or you can

convert an old sink (see Chapter 4).

★ *Circular bowls* These make excellent focal points when planted up thickly with spring flowers and bulbs or summer bedding.

★ *Novelty containers* There is still plenty of scope for originality, using objects ranging from wheelbarrows and tyres to tin helmets and chimney pots.

★ *Barrels and multipots* Wooden or plastic barrels, with holes cut in the sides, are eyecatching when planted with spring or summer bedding, or rock plants. They become functional as well as decorative when used for growing strawberries. Multi/tower pots also come in handy for growing a few choice herbs. Buy purpose-made barrels or improvise with redundant wine casks.

★ *Self-watering containers* Relatively

This old sink has been re-cycled – and re-sited – to become a plant container.

new, these are inclined to be expensive. Self-watering containers can be of great benefit in summer, but a disaster in winter, when excess water can quickly kill a plant.

Planting containers When planting in containers it is just as important to consider the needs of plants as when planting anywhere else in the garden. Consider not only the amount of sun or shade and exposure to wind, but also the suitability of plant containers and composts. To help you choose wisely, consult the lists in this chapter and in chapters 4 and 6.

The time to plant is crucial and varies according to what you are planting. Summer bedding should be planted in late May, after the last frost, to give colour from June to October. Spring bedding is usually planted in September/October, after summer bedding has

Spring bedding plants for container growing

Name	Habit	Position	Nature of interest	Treatment
Arabis Rock cress	Spreading, low	○	Pink or white flowers	HB-HP
Bellis Double daisy	Rosette, short	○ ◑	Pink, red or white flowers	HB
Cheiranthus Wallflower, Siberian wallflower	Bushy, short to tall	○	Gold, red, maroon, orange or cream scented flowers	HB
Hyacinthus Hyacinth	Upright, medium	○ ◑	Blue, pink, red or white fragrant flower	HBb
Iberis Perennial candytuft	Low, bushy	○	White flowers	HB/HP
Matthiola Brompton stock	Upright, medium to tall	○	Blue, pink, mauve, red, purple or white scented flowers	HB
Narcissus Daffodil/narcissus	Upright, short to tall	○ ◑	Gold, orange, white or bicoloured flowers; some scented	HBb
Primula Auricula, Polyanthus, Primrose	Rosette, short to medium	◑ ●	Bicoloured, mixed flowers; some scented	HB/HP
Tulipa Bedding tulips	Upright, short to tall	○	Pink, red, white, gold, orange or bicoloured flowers	HBb
Viola Pansy/viola	Compact, bushy	○ ◑	Blue, gold, red or white flowers; some scented	HB

Primula

Cheiranthus

Matthiola

been cleared away, to bloom from February to May. Trees, shrubs and climbers, including conifers and other evergreens, are best planted in autumn or spring. Spring-flowering perennials are planted in autumn, and summer and autumn-flowering perennials in spring.

Planting in a container

Drainage Ensure that containers have plenty of drainage holes in the bottom;

this is very important for outdoor plants, which are exposed to rain. Cover the container bottom with gauze to keep out mice and to stop the compost being washed out. Cover the mesh with a layer of pebbles, pieces of broken polystyrene or broken clay flower pots (crocks). Omit this layer for self-watering pots. Be sure to puncture the undersides of growbags.

Potting composts For windowboxes, tubs and troughs a good soil-based

compost is easiest to manage. John Innes No 2 potting compost is excellent and suitable for a very wide range of plants. But use ericaceous acid potting composts for lime haters like azaleas, camellias and rhododendrons. Use peat-based composts for hanging baskets and containers where weight is the main priority. Avoid using ordinary garden soil; it compacts badly, gives poor drainage and poor growth, and it is also highly likely to harbour troublesome pests and diseases.

Summer bedding for container growing

Name	Habit	Position	Nature of interest	Treatment
Ageratum Floss flower	Low, bushy	○	Blue or white flowers	HHA
Alyssum Sweet alyssum	Compact, bushy	○ ◑	Pink, purple or white scented flowers	HHA
Begonia Fibrous/tuberous begonias	Bushy, tufted or pendulous	○ ◑	Orange, pink, red, yellow or white flowers	HHA/HHBb
Calceolaria Slipper flower	Low, bushy	○ ◑	Yellow flowers	HHA/HHP
Campanula isophylla Italian bellflower	Trailing or spreading	○ ◑	Blue or white flowers	HHA/HHP
Fuchsia Fuchsia	Bushy or pendulous	○ ◑	Pink, red, purple, white or bicoloured flowers	HHP
Gazania Treasure flower	Low, bushy	○	Cream, red, yellow or white flowers	HHA
Hedera Ivy	Climbing or trailing	○ ◑ ●	Green or variegated evergreen leaves	HP/HHP
Heliotropium Cherry Pie	Bushy, short to tall	○	Purple fragrant flowers	HHA/HHP
Impatiens Busy lizzie	Bushy, short to tall	○ ◑	Pink, purple, red, white, orange or bicoloured flowers	HHA/HHP
Kochia Burning bush	Tall, bushy	○ ◑	Ferny green foliage turning red in in autumn	HHA
Lobelia Lobelia	Bushy or trailing	○ ◑	Blue, carmine or white flowers	HHA
Lysimachia Creeping Jennie	Trailing	○ ◑	Yellow flowers	HHP/HP
Matthiola 10-week stock	Compact, upright	○	Pink, purple, cream, red, blue or white scented flowers	HHA
Pelargonium Bedding geranium Ivy-leaved geranium	 Bushy Trailing	 ○ ○	Pink, red, maroon, white or bicoloured flowers	HHA/HHP HHP
Petunia Petunia	Bushy	○	Pink, purple, red, yellow, white or bicoloured scented flowers	HHA
Salvia Salvia	Bushy	○	Pink, purple, scarlet or white flowers	HHA
Tagetes French marigold, African marigold	Bushy	○ ◑	Gold, orange, bronze, mahogany or bicoloured flowers	HHA
Thunbergia Black-eyed Susan	Climbing or trailing	○	Orange, yellow or white flowers, with or without black eye	HHA
Tropaeolum Nasturtium	Bushy or trailing	○	Gold, orange or red flowers	HH/HHA
Viola Pansy/viola	Low, bushy	○ ◑ ●	Blue, gold, purple, or white flowers; some scented	HHA/HHB

Note: For lists of trees, shrubs, climbers and perennials suitable for containers, see Chapter 6, and for suitable rock plants, see Chapter 4

sphagnum moss

potting compost

polythene

A traditional hanging basket lined with moss. Details of its construction are shown left.

Filling Cover the pebbles, polystyrene or 'crocks' with a thin layer of damp peat. After you have done this, partially fill the container with a potting compost mixture.

Planting Water all plants thoroughly and allow to drain before carefully easing them out of their containers. To plant singly, spread the roots in the centre on a cushion of compost, with the top of the rootball 2.5cm (1in) or so below the rim. Work damp compost into the space between rootball and container, firming as the filling proceeds. Cover the top of the rootball with 1-2cm (½-¾in) of compost, still leaving space for watering. Water thoroughly after planting.

If several plants are being set out in one container, such as a windowbox, be sure to follow the 'tallest-behind-the-shortest' rule. If a container is backed against a wall, place the taller plants towards the back and the shortest towards the front. Those containers viewed from two sides should have the tallest plants in a row in the middle. In the case of round containers or hanging baskets, place the tallest plants in the centre. Set out the tallest plants first, working compost around the roots and ending with all the plants set slightly deeper than before the move, but with the roots well covered.

Hanging baskets Support the basket in a bucket. Line the basket with a foam plastic liner with vertical slits, then plant, starting from the bottom. Gently work the roots of small plants, such as lobelia, from the outside inwards, through the mesh and a slit in the foam, leaving the foliage, flowers and buds exposed. Cover the roots with compost as filling proceeds, and, finally, plant the top as described previously.

Modern baskets, with solid plastic sides, are planted in the top only, as are wire baskets if fibre liners are used. The traditional lining of baskets was moss, but this is being used less and less.

Sink gardens Crock and partially fill as for planters, then ignore the 'tallest-behind-the-shortest' rule. Plant one or two dwarf conifers of contrasting shape and size, well apart, surround with small rock plants and alpines. Add some pieces of rock for effect, as planting proceeds. The alternative is to plunge plant. Leave all the plants in their pots and simply plunge the pots up to their rims in compost or peat. This makes it easier to change planting schemes, but demands closer attention to watering and annual re-potting.

Barrels Success with barrels calls for good watering and adequate ventilation. Stand the barrel on well drained gravel. Make a 5-8cm (2-3in) diameter cylinder of small mesh wire, as tall as the barrel is high. Set this wire column vertically in the centre, and fill it with small, clean pebbles. Plant up the sides in much the same way as for hanging baskets. Water by pouring down the pebble column.

Aftercare

Permanent container plants are going to need re-potting at least every other year, and topping up with fresh compost in the interim.

Chapter 4

GARDEN FEATURES

One very important part of garden making is to exploit the visual qualities of the site. The art is to hide the defects and focus attention on the better features. As always, the keys are planning and knowing not only your site, but also all the options available. In this chapter we discusss some of the many approaches open to you.

When well-constructed and planted imaginatively, rock gardens, in one form or another, rarely fail to arouse interest. Ways and means of making island outcrops and rocky banks are discussed. There are hardy rock and alpine plants to suit most situations – whether in sun or shade.

Even the faintest glint of sun will sparkle in the clear water of a garden pool. We discuss suitable pools and also simple methods of construction. In no time you could be resting to the sound of moving water from a waterfall of your own creation!

Focal points

Few will deny the pleasure and satisfaction to be gained from a garden. The differences of opinion arise when it comes to rating priorities: growing a particularly difficult plant; harvesting choice fruit and vegetables; or maybe just feeling fitter after an hour or two hoeing and digging. Inevitably, however, it is the visual quality of a garden – its beauty or otherwise – that has the greatest impact.

Gardens are composed of a collection of features, good as well as bad, and part of the art of garden design is to exploit the good and camouflage the less favourable. Focal points help, by diverting attention to what is best. A focal point can be a strategically placed bird-bath or sundial; a pool or fountain; a colourful flower bed or a fine specimen shrub or tree. It is the siting and treatment which are all important.

Tricks of the trade The following few simple rules provide the key to success.
★ *Avoid clutter* Resist the temptation to have more than one focal point from any one viewing position. A number of focal points, seen at the same time, serve only to clutter the scene and compete with each other for attention.
★ *Frame the view* Try to frame the view of substantial focal points. Rock gardens, pools or fountains, for example, become even more important when seen through an archway, an opening in a wall or fence, or a pair of flanking tall conifers.
★ *Provide a background* An alternative to framing is to provide a hedge or quiet background, enclosing the view within the garden.
★ *Use vistas and paths* In a long, narrow garden it is not uncommon for paths to be straight, providing a line of vision from one end to the other. The views at the ends of the paths often terminate in a blank wall or in some other equally uninspiring way. Frequently, these are

This outcrop rock garden setting uses limestone blocks.

suitable spots to site pieces of statuary, or perhaps a colourful tub or urn of flowers. In many older gardens, cross paths are found intersecting the main path. Make these intersections into attractive focal points by the provision of a bird-bath, sundial, small formal pool or other feature.

The typical Japanese garden conforms to very definite rules about the use of colour and the position of major focal points. Basically, the rules state that the focal point should have a simple but effective foreground, like water, sand or grass, with a definite but subdued background of trees or distant objects like mountains or sky. In the modern, small garden, many of these ideas can be adapted. A colourful specimen shrub or flower bed, with a foreground of grass – or maybe the paving of courtyard or patio – and backed by a hedge or greenery, can create a pleasing picture.

Rock gardens

A rock garden can become an outstanding attraction as well as an absorbing hobby. It is not difficult to gradually build up a collection of dwarf, slow-growing rock and alpine plants which will put on a good show for most of the year.

Among the most popular variations on the rock garden theme are island outcrops, rock-strewn banks and planted retaining walls; the latter two provide a useful link between different levels. And many rock garden plants will grow happily in spaces left in paving. Peat walls and raised beds offer further scope, especially if your interest is primarily in specialist plants or if the surrounding soil is unsuitable for rock and alpine plants. Initially, a rock garden can prove expensive, especially if you import rock from some distance

away. Once constructed, however, it should last a lifetime. If a rock garden is neglected, though, and allowed to become overgrown with weeds, a fair amount of work is involved if it is to be put right.

Making a rockery

Site Select an open position; avoid heavily shaded areas and the drip of overhanging trees. An east or west aspect is deal for many plants in warm southern districts. In the north and in cold, exposed gardens, planting pockets are best facing south. If you are lucky and have a natural slope, exploit this.

Preparations Fork out weeds, apply weedkiller if necessary. It is better to delay planting and have a clean start, than a never-ending battle against perennial weeds. Good drainage is critical, especially on clay soils and in low-lying gardens. In these circumstances, the construction of a rubble-filled soakaway near the base of the planned rockery is a wise precaution, as is excavating and building the island rockery over 10cm (4in) of rubble.

Choosing the stone If possible, buy local stone to save on haulage. Generally, sandstone and limestone are the two most widely available. It is unwise to mix stones of different types; they always look uncomfortable. Concrete and imitation stone are the most difficult to use successfully, as they tend to look raw. Treating them with sulphate of iron helps to give a weathered look. Whatever stone you use, go for a variation in size. Rounded or flat stones are difficult to place; rectangular stones are easier. Avoid very small pieces of stone or your rock garden will resemble a heap of rubble rather than a natural outcrop. Avoid using too much stone; a few well chosen rocks often give the best results, with the odd large boulder adding character.

Laying the stone Placing the weathered side uppermost, set the rocks at the same angle throughout, to resemble layers of strata found in mountainous districts. A simple rockery can be made by embedding stones in level soil, but it is not as satisfactory as a raised feature.

Island rockery To avoid an unnatural humpy effect, the width of the bed should be at least four or five times the height of the rocks in the centre. Start at the lower, outer edge, burying the largest stones to a third their depth in excavated hollows. Pack and ram round with soil. Test each stone for firmness

Set rocks at an angle for a south- or southwest-facing planting area.

before moving on to the next, and resetting if there is any sign of wobble. Build up the soil in 15cm (6in) consolidated layers. A useful source of soil would be from the construction of a pool at the same time. Add an inner course or courses of stone to form a central plateau, with planting pockets on all sides. Fill these with a mixture of two parts John Innes No 2 to one part grit.

Banks Banks are usually best when terraced, and this becomes structurally necessary on slopes steeper than 1 in 2. Pleasing effects on shallow slopes are possible by the random arrangement of stones. Again, start at the bottom of the bank with the largest stones and work systematically up the incline.

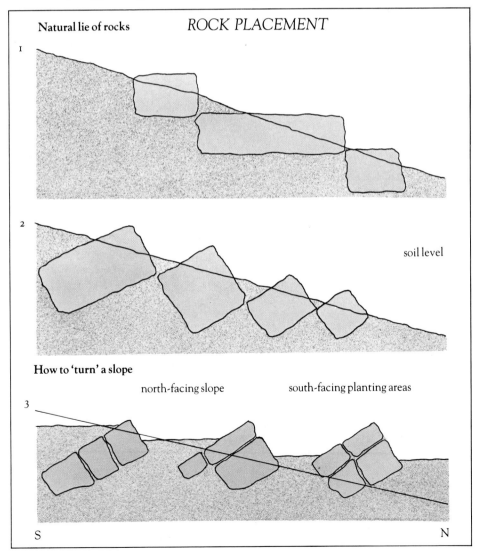

ROCK PLACEMENT

Natural lie of rocks
1

2
soil level

How to 'turn' a slope
north-facing slope   south-facing planting areas
3

S   N

Rock garden plants

Name	Habit	Position	Soil	Nature	Season of interest
Achillea vars Alpine yarrow	Hummock or mat, compact, E	○	N C	HP	Gold or white flowers in summer
Alyssum saxatile Gold dust	Low mound, E	○	N C	HP	Gold scented flowers in spring
Arabis albida 'Snowflake'	Spreading, E	○ ◑	A N C	P	White flowers in spring
Aquilegia flabellata Columbine	Erect, spreading	○ ◑	A	P	White flowers turning to purple in summer
Armeria caespitosa Thrift	Compact mound, E	○	A N C	P	Pink flowers in late spring
Aubrieta various Purple rock cress	Carpeting, E	○	N C	HP	Blue, pink, purple, red or mauve flowers in spring
Campanula various Bellflower	Spreading, D, E	○ ○	N C	HP	Blue or white flowers in summer
Conifers various	Low growing or spreading, E	○ ◑	A N C	HSh	Blue, gold, green, grey or variegated foliage
Cotoneaster dammeri	Prostrate, E	○ ●	A N C	HSh	White flowers in summer, red berries in autumn and winter
Crocus various	Grassy, bulbous, D	○	N	HBb	Blue, gold, purple or white flowers in spring
Cytisus × beanii Broom	Prostrate or low growing, D	○	N	HSh	Cream, gold or pink flowers in spring and early summer
Daphne dwarf vars	Bushy, D, E	○	A N C	HSh	Pink or reddish purple scented flowers in spring
Dianthus alpinus Pink	Dense hummocks	○ ◑	C	P	Pink/purple flowers in summer
Erica carnea vars Winter-flowering heather	Bushy or mounded, E	○	A N C	HSh	Pink, purple, red or white flowers in winter and spring
Ferns dwarf vars	Erect clumps or rosettes, D, E	○ ●	A N C	HP	Finely divided green summer foliage
Genista 'Lydia' Broom	Stiffly arching, bushy, carpeting, D	○	N	HSh	Yellow flowers in late spring and early summer
Gentiana acaulis Trumpet Gentian	Prostrate, spreading	○ ◑	A	P	Deep blue flowers in summer
Geranium dwarf vars	Hummock or spreading, D	○ ◑	N	HP	Pink, purple or blue flowers in summer
Gypsophila repens vars Baby's breath	Hummock, D	○	N C	HP	Pink or white flowers in summer
Helianthemum named vars Sun rose	Shrubby, E	○	N	HSh	Bronze, gold, pink or red flowers in summer
Hypericum dwarf vars St John's Wort	Trailing, mat and mound forming, D, E	○ ◑	A N C	HP	Yellow flowers in summer
Iberis 'Snowflake' Candytuft	Prostrate or shrubby, E	○ ◑	N C	HSh	White flowers in spring
Lavandula dwarf vars Lavender	Bushy, E	○	N C	HSh	Lavender, blue, violet, pink or white aromatic flowers in summer

Rock garden plants

Name	Habit	Position	Soil	Nature	Season of interest
Linum flavum Flax	Erect mass of slender stems, D	○	N	HP	Blue or gold flowers in summer
Lychnis alpina syn. *Viscaria alpina* Campion	Tufted	○ ◑	N	P	Deep rose pink flowers in summer
Myosotis alpestris Forget-me-not	Erect stems, bushy	○	A N C	HP	Sky blue flowers in early summer. Fragrant
Narcissus bulbocodium Daffodil/narcissi	Clump, D	○ ◑	A N C	HBd	Gold, orange, bicoloured or white flowers. Some scented
Oenothera pumila Evening primrose	Trailing or mat forming, D	○	N	HP	Yellow flowers in summer
Papaver alpinum Poppy	Slightly arching slender stems, low mounds	○	N	P (treat as annual)	White, yellow, red or orange flowers in mid-summer
Phlox various Alpine phlox	Prostrate or trailing, D, E	○	N C	HP	Blue, pink, mauve or white flowers in summer
Potentilla various Dwarf cinquefoil	Tufty, trailing or spreading, D	○	N C	HP	Gold, orange or white flowers in summer
Primula various Alpine primula	Rosette forming, D, E	○ ◑	N	HP	Gold, pink, red, purple, orange, white or bicoloured flowers in spring and summer
Saponaria ocymoides	Prostrate	○	N	HP	Vivid pink flowers in late summer
Saxifraga various Dwarf saxifrage	Mounded or mat forming, E	○ ◑	N C	HP	Gold, pink, red or white flowers in spring and summer
Thymus various Thyme	Bushy or mat forming, E	○	N C	HSh	Pink, red or white flowers in late spring and summer
Tiarella cordifolia Foam flower	Creeping, S-E	○	N	HP	White feathery flowers in summer
Tulipa species Dwarf tulips	Clump forming, D	○	N	HBb	Various shades of flowers in spring
Viola cornuta vars Viola	Spreading or tufted, E	○ ◑	N	HB/HP	Amber, gold, violet or white flowers in spring and summer

See also Chapter 3, Edging and paving plants, page 38

Campanula

Helianthemum

Hypericum

Walls When building, leave planting pockets in the sides and top, in which rock plants will thrive.

Paving See Chapter 3.

Choosing plants

Devote at least half the planted area to evergreens, such as dwarf conifers, and you will be sure to have year-round interest. Choose flowering plants carefully to give a succession of colour throughout the year. Don't forget to match your plants with site and soil conditions, unless you are prepared to give them a good deal of nursing. Ignore any plants which are not pot grown. As well as the following list, see the list in Chapter 3 of plants for edging and paving.

Planting rock garden and alpine plants

Preparation Plant after all the rocks are firmly in place and settled. September and October are good months in the warm, sheltered areas. In cold, wet areas, spring planting is best. Water the plants and planting pockets a few hours beforehand. Set the plants a fraction deeper than before the move, to allow for a thin scattering of fine chippings. Use limestone chippings for the majority of plants, and granite chippings for lime haters. Water gently to settle.

Siting Position larger plants, such as dwarf conifers, in prominent places; at the base of a rock and in the recesses between stones are ideal. Infill 'by eye' with trailers and carpeters, but ensure that some are planted at the top of rocks to tumble over the edges, and some are planted in the joints where they help to prevent soil erosion. Rosette formers such as sedum are best set into crevices, especially in areas of high rainfall, where water standing in the rosettes encourages rotting.

Island rockeries Start in the centre and plant out towards the edges.

Banks Start at the top and gradually work down, to lessen the risk of plants being damaged by falling debris.

Walls Line a crevice with damp compost. Wrap the roots of a young rock plant in moist peat, and work the roots well back into the crevice so that they make contact with the compost lining. Pack with more compost until securely wedged.

Instant effect Bury pots of alpine or rock plants up to their rims, after first covering the drainage holes with fine gauze to keep out soil pests.
Where the soil is below par, sink plants in their pots. The plants need to be lifted and re-potted each year.

Garden Pools

Use modern methods and materials, and the job of making a small garden pool can be tackled in a weekend. Though it takes relatively little time to

The Aethionem armenum 'Warley Rose' is an exquisite perennial for walls. It needs a well-drained sunny site.

install, you should spend some time thinking about the type of pool you want, and its position in the garden.

Site and size A sunny spot is best. Avoid overhanging trees which are likely to foul the water with their falling leaves.

If fish are included in your scheme, aim for a minimum surface area of 1.4sq m (15sq ft). Fish need a minimum depth of 38cm (15in); a depth of 45cm (18in) is better, and adequate for a range of deep aquatics. In a very shallow pool, there is a risk of water freezing solid in winter; at other times the temperature tends to fluctuate badly – good for neither fish nor plants.

Materials Before making a choice, weigh up carefully the appearance, cost, ease of installation and maintenance implications.
★ *Concrete* creates a feeling of permanence, but it is not the easiest material to handle. It is heavy; shuttering needs

to be erected; 'free' lime needs to be neutralised; and a sealant is needed to make the pool watertight. Any one of the following modern lining materials is better for first timers:

★ *Glass fibre* Pools in this material are marketed in a standard range of shapes and sizes, up to about 2.4m (8ft) in length. Preformed, they are easy to install, and should last for twenty years or more.

★ *Moulded plastic* A bit cheaper than glass fibre and similar in many respects, moulded plastic pools have a lifespan of about ten years.

★ *Flexible liners* Within reason, these enable pools of any shape and size to be made. Butyl rubber, often guaranteed up to fifteen years, is the most permanent material. Next comes nylon reinforced twin-skin plastic, which lasts up to ten years. Standard twin-skin liners are likely to need replacing after about three years. Single skin liners are obviously much less durable and only intended for temporary use.

Making a pool

Shape With moulded liners this is predetermined. With flexible liners, keep things simple; go for sweeping curves. Consider having a shelved area of shallow water near the pool edge, for growing marginal plants.

First, peg out the area, perhaps creating a rock garden or water course nearby to take up excavated soil. Skim off any turf, and dig out the hole with sides sloping 20°, to avoid subsidence later. Make provision for shelving, cut out any tree roots, and remove all loose, sharp stones. Ram firmly afterwards to consolidate the whole area. Check for size, allowing for a 5cm (2in) gap all round with moulded liners. Before bedding any liner, spread a 5cm (2in) layer of wet sand over the entire area.

Moulded liners Work into position, packing with sand to firm and level. Check with a straightedge and spirit level; this is important because water will escape from any low points, and the level surface of the water will draw attention to the uneven rim of the pool.

Flexible liners Spread the liner over the pool area, weighting down the edges all round with bricks. Gradually fill the pool, allowing the weight of water to settle the liner into position. Trim round the edge, leaving about 15cm (6in) overlap to tuck under the surround.

The surround is a matter of personal preference, and can be formal or informal. Paving slabs which have been laid over a bed of sand are practical; they need to overhang the pool by about 5cm (2in) to conceal the liner. Other alternatives include bringing lawns, bog gardens or rockeries up to the water's edge.

Cascades and waterfalls are best constructed at the same time as pools.

A GARDEN POOL

A water garden is as simple or as complicated as you wish. You can choose pre-shaped one- or two-level pools (below) and use lights (right), ornaments (right below) or even waterfalls or sprays as you wish.

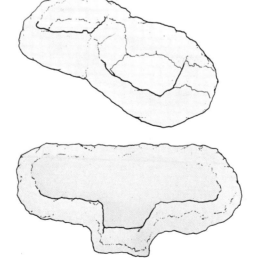

Pool plants

Marginal plants for shallow water

Name	Water depth	Height	Position	Feature/season
Acorus calamus 'Variegatus' Sweet flag	3-13cm 1-5in	60-75cm 2-2½ft	○ ◑	Green and cream leaves in summer
Alisma plantago Water plantain	3-15cm 1-6in	15-30cm 6-12in	○	Pink flowers in summer
Butomus umbellatus Flowering rush	8-13cm 3-5in	60-120cm 2-4ft	○	Pink flowers in summer
Caltha palustris vars Marsh marigold	1-10cm ½-4in	20-40cm 8-16in	○	Mainly gold or white spring flowers
Eriophorum angustifolium Cotton grass	1-8cm ½-3in	30-45cm 12-18in	○	Cotton-wool-like tufts in summer
Hypericum eloides Marsh hypericum	1-5cm ½-2in	15-30cm 6-12in	○ ◐	Pale yellow flowers in summer
Iris *laevigata* Japanese iris	 3-13cm 1-5in	 60-75cm 2-2½ft	 ○	 Blue flowers in summer
pseudacorus Yellow flag	5-40cm 2-16in	60-90cm 2-3ft	○	Yellow flowers in May-June
Juncus effusus 'Spiralis' Corkscrew rush	3-15cm 1-6in	45cm 18in	○ ◑	Curious spiralled grassy stems, brown flowers in summer
Menyanthes trifoliata Bog bean	3-10cm 1-4in	30cm 12in	○	Pink flowers in summer
Mimulus various Musk/Monkey flower	0-10cm 0-4in	15-45cm 6-18in	○ ◑	Gold, pink, red or orange flowers in late spring and summer
Myosotis palustris Water forget-me-not	0-5cm 0-2in	15-20cm 6-8in	○ ◑	Bright blue flowers in summer

Fountains and lighting can be installed once the pool is firmly in place.

Choice of plants Be wary of plant gifts; beetles, weeds and disease are all easily introduced. When choosing plants for a pool, consider their function as well as their appearance, and make sure your pool can offer the depth of water they need in order to thrive.

★ *Deep-water aquatics* The roots of these ornamental plants anchor at depth, and the leaves rest on the surface, affording valuable shade.

★ *Oxygenating plants* These feed on mineral salts, and provide shady pockets, starving out harmful algae. They breathe out oxygen, vital to fish, and provide their food and shelter.

★ *Floaters* provide shade as they rise and

Name	Water depth	Height	Position	Feature/season
Orontium aquaticum Golden club	3-20cm 1-8in	30-45cm 12-18in	○	Gold spikes in summer
Pontederia cordata Pickerel weed	10-20cm 4-8in	45-120cm 18-48in	○	Blue flower spikes in summer
Ranunculus lingua Spearwort	10-25cm 4-10in	60-90cm 2-3ft	○	Gold flowers in late spring and early summer
Sagittaria sagittifolia Arrowhead	5-15cm 2-6in	30-45cm 12-18in	○	White flowers in summer
Scirpus 'Zebrinus' Zebra rush	5-15cm 2-6in	60-90cm 2-3ft	○ ◑	Green and white barred stems
Veronica beccabunga Brooklime	0-8cm 0-3in	15-20cm 6-18in	○ ◑	Blue flowers in summer
Zantedeschia 'Crowborough' Arum lily	10-25cm 4-10in	60-90cm 2-3ft	○ ◑	White flowers in summer

Acorus calamus

Caltha palustris

Iris pseudacorus

fall with prevailing conditions; they guarantee spawning grounds and food for fish.

★ *Marginal plants* provide colour, shade for fish and cover for snails.

★ *Bog plants* make an excellent visual transition from garden to pond.

★ *Livestock* Fish are a must, if practical, not only for their aesthetic value, but because they devour larvae, aphids and submerged vegetation. In their absence, consider water fleas, which feed on algae and do part of the job. Snails clean the water by feeding on decaying remains, but use recommended species

A delightful pond in which careful use has also been made of waterside plants. Note the Iris kaemferi to the right. This thrives in moist but not wet soil.

only; some snails breed rapidly and can become unwelcome pests.

Achieving a balance Don't overstock the pool with plants or wildlife. The surface needs to be a third to half covered with vegetation, to discourage the growth of algae, but no more, or oxygenating plants are starved of light and the pool balance is upset. As a guide, one water lily, five oxygenating plants, four marginals, two floaters and six snails would be adequate to stock a pool with a surface area of 1.4sq m (15sq ft). When all is in harmony, the pool is clear. The recommendation for fish is one fish (approximately 5cm [2in] long) per 42sq cm (2sq ft) of pond area. A 1.4sq m (15sq ft) pond could take up to nine fish.

Planting the pool

If deep-water aquatics are bought as established plants in baskets, they can be planted at most times of year, otherwise aquatics are best planted when in active growth – usually between May and August. This gives the plants time to become established by winter.

The bottom of the pool can be covered with a layer of soil, then topped with gravel and planted up directly, but this is not recommended. Plants run riot, and fish muddy the water. It is best to use containers; they curb spreaders, and allow for plant re-arrangement and a complete clean out. With containers, planting is easier, less soil is needed and fish don't stir up clouds of mud. Baskets must be lined with hessian first, to prevent the soil being washed out. Plant one kind of plant per basket and cover with washed chippings.

Don't immerse plants to the full depth immediately. Place the plants just below the surface, raised up on bricks; lower the plants gradually to the recommended depth of water over a period of several weeks. Let the water of a newly filled pool mature for a few days before introducing plants.

Immediately after planting, the water will turn green and cloudy. This is natural, but it should clear after a few weeks. Add a few extra oxygenating plants to speed things up; be prepared to thin them out later. Introduce the fish when the water has cleared.

Soil Use heavy soil. Don't add peat, garden compost or leaf mould, or mineral salts will dissolve out, encourage algae and pollute the pool. They also produce toxins dangerous to fish. The only fertilisers recommended are sachets of water plant fertiliser. Apply before planting, according to the manufacturer's instructions.

Planting use wet soil and plant deep aquatics firmly. Leave the crowns of

Floating plants for any depth of water

Name	Notes
Azolla caroliniana Fairy floating moss	Ferny green foliage turns red in autumn. Frost tender; overwinter in water indoors. Spreads quickly
Eichornia crassipes Water hyacinth	Violet and gold flowers in summer. Half hardy; put outdoors in June, bring indoors in September.
Hydrocharis morsus-ranae Frogbit	Hardy. Non-invasive. White flowers in summer.
Stratiotes aloides Water soldier	Rosettes of spiky green leaves, partly submerged. White flowers in summer. Hardy.
Trapa natans Water chestnut	Floating annual. Seeds germinate in spring to produce curious triangular green leaves. Flowers inconspicuous.

Submerged oxygenators

Name	Water depth	Notes
Callitriche autumnale Water starwort	15-40cm 6-16in	Hardy, produces white starry flowers when leaves reach the surface in summer.
Ceratophyllum demersum Hornwort	30-75cm 12-30in	Excellent for cold, deep water.
Elodea canadensis Canadian pond weed	15-60cm 6-24in	Hardy, and can become invasive.
Fontinalis antipyretica Willow moss	15-40cm 6-16in	Excellent oxygenators. Good for fish.
Hottonia palustris Water violet	15-25in 6-10in	Hardy. Lilac, carmine flowers in summer. Plants disappear in winter.
Myriophyllum spicatum Milfoil	15-60cm 6-24in	Vigorous; quick to establish. Small crimson flowers.
Ranunculus aquatilis Water crowfoot	15-30cm 6-12in	Hardy. White flowers in spring.

Note: These plants need sun

water lilies just above the soil surface. Oxygenators are often planted as unrooted cuttings in baskets, burying the cut ends to a depth of 1cm (½in). Marginals are firmly planted in baskets. Floaters are dropped into the pool to establish themselves at or just below the surface. Bog plants are planted directly into damp patches along the edge.

Fountains and waterfalls

Moving water looks good, and the splash of water raises the oxygen level, which is of enormous benefit to fish in thundery weather. Moving water also prevents dust settling, and goes a long way to prevent the rampant growth of algae. A fountain or waterfall may bring a pool to life, but moving water lowers the temperature of the pool (important early and late in the year), and many aquatics resent fast-flowing water or turbulence.

Tricks of the trade If you still find the thought of a fountain or waterfall alluring, and are determined to have either one or both in your garden, you should

Deep water aquatics

Name	Water depth	Position	Colour/season	Notes
Aponogeton Water hawthorn	15-45cm 6-18in	○ ◑	White flowers in spring to autumn	Hardy; scented.
Nuphar Yellow water lily	60-120cm 2-4ft	○ ◑	Yellow flowers in summer	Too vigorous for small pools.
Nymphaea various Water lily strong growers medium growers small/miniature	45-90cm 18-36in 30-60cm 12-24in 20-30cm 8-12in	○	Gold, pink, red or white flowers in summer	Select varieties to suit pool depth and size. Protect miniatures from frost.
Nymphoides peltata Water fringe	15-30cm 6-12in	○	Yellow flowers in summer	Spreads readily.
Villarsia reniformis	10-45cm 4-18in	○	Yellow flowers in summer	Hardy in warm districts only.

Stratiotes aloides

Elodea canadensis

Aponogeton

keep the following points in mind:
★ *Use moving water cautiously* during early spring and late autumn, when temperatures can be low. Disconnect the system during winter.
★ *Keep fountains well away from aquatics* In small pools use those mounted at the sides to spray water back into the pool.
★ *Always recirculate water taken from the pool* Never draw water from a cold tap and create a flow-through system. It is a fantastic waste of water, and the water used never gets a chance to mature properly. In practice, water is recirculated by an electric pump – installation must be carried out by a qualified electrician.
★ *Provide a wind screen* Spray drift can be a problem, for both nearby plants and people.

Waterfalls look best in a rock garden. There are 'mix and match' moulded water courses available, which are installed singly or in combination. Moulded rock pools are ideal for setting near (but not at) the top of the rockery, as the header for a waterfall. Moulded rock streams can extend the length of the course, and moulded waterfalls and cascades can be used to tumble the water into the pool. These are installed as for the pool. Remember that the delivery hose from the pump to the header pool needs to be buried alongside the water course. Soften the appearance of the edges of moulded water courses with rocks, pebbles and plants, but don't set the plants within the water flow. Shallow rock pools are not intended for aquatic life. Flexible liners can create a more natural effect than moulded water courses, but the flexible liners can also be extremely tricky to position.

Chapter 5

SOIL CARE

In order to achieve a fertile, well-managed soil, thorough pre-planting and pre-sowing preparations are vital if you are to avoid disappointments. So this chapter deals with ways of ridding the ground of weeds, simple soil drainage and sound soil cultivation. In addition, it looks at such questions as digging versus rotary cultivators and whether or not manure should be dug in.

Advice is given on good manuring practice and liming. Regular applications of farmyard manure or garden compost are necessary to build up and maintain soil fertility. But well-made garden compost is just as good and can easily be made in any garden by following the guidelines given.

The vast majority of plants benefit from feeding with concentrated fertilizers. And these are discussed – along with the various methods of application – as dry fertilizers, or liquid root drenches or foliar feeds.

The importance of soil preparation

If garden plants are to grow and crop well and build up a resistance to pests and diseases, a strong and vigorous root system is essential. This enables them to obtain from the soil most of the moisture and nutrients needed, and to provide stable anchorage. The quality of the root environment is determined by how the soil is managed. Good soil management is a continuous process of building up and subsequently maintaining fertility.

Thorough soil preparations before sowing and planting get underway are easier and quicker than when the borders are full of plants. Clean land gets seedlings and young plants off to a good start; skimping on the preparatory work is likely to inflict subsequent starvation, suffering and setback. In this chapter we look at the jobs which need to be done.

Ground clearance

Whether dealing with an existing border or fresh ground, first clear off surface debris, including rubbish and weeds. Work when the land is not too wet, and try to be finished by autumn so the land is ready for sowing or planting the following spring. Fork up deep-rooted weeds and those setting seed, taking care not to spread the seeds. Dispose of these remains, rather than composting, or you risk spreading weeds when distributing the compost. Fork out spent crops. Burn woody and diseased remains, and compost soft, healthy leaves and stems.

★ *Using weed-killer* If the ground is riddled with deep-rooted, difficult weeds such as ground elder, creeping buttercup, convolvulus and couch grass, weed-killer is more practical than hand weeding. Use a systemic weed-killer, when the weeds are growing freely, and take care there is no drift to nearby valuable plants. Systemic chemicals are carried in the sap down to the roots, and are much more effective than contact weed-killers, which kill off top growth only. Use as directed, leaving the ground vacant until all traces of weed-killer have gone; this usually takes from three to six months. Test if the border is safe before planting, by sowing small quantities of radish seed any time between March and October. If no seedlings appear in 21 days, sow again, and only set out plants after the emergence of seedlings. See Chapter 9 for more details about weed-killers.

Draining wet ground

Very wet ground is useless for the majority of garden plants, as roots suffocate and die. If in doubt, test your soil as described on pages 12-13. Clays are usually slow draining and most in need of help. A practical way to drain wet ground in a small garden is by building rubble-filled sumps.

★ *Making a sump drain* Site sump drains in low, wet spots, and carry out the job

It is essential to clear your ground thoroughly before preparing soil.

in dry weather. Dig out a hole about 75cm (2½ft) square and 90cm (3ft) deep. Stack any good topsoil on one side, and remove the sub-soil. Fill the hole to within 30cm (12in) of the surface with clean rubble, tamping firm as filling proceeds. Cover the rubble with a 2.5cm (1in) layer of fine chippings, to stop the soil being washed down. Level off up to the surface with topsoil. A single sump drain can drain an area up to 5-6m sq (17-20ft sq), depending on soil conditions.

Digging

Why dig? There is no more effective way of breaking in fresh land, nor of preparing cultivated land for sowing or planting, than to dig with a spade. Digging is invaluable, too, for cleaning up beds and borders.

During digging, small weeds are buried, weed growth on the surface is eliminated, at least temporarily, and the roots of perennial weeds can easily be removed. Harmful grubs and insects are exposed, then devoured by birds. Digging relieves soil compaction; root development and penetration is made easier and so the drought resistance of plants is improved. Aeration is increased, which enables soil to warm up more quickly in spring, and enables water to percolate more freely. Exposing fresh soil to the elements allows the beneficial effects of weathering to improve the soil texture. Digging allows you to work manure and garden compost into the soil, to improve and maintain soil fertility. Frequent digging, however, without the addition of organic matter inevitably leads to a poor soil.

When to dig Digging of vacant ground and land recently cleared of crops is normally best done in autumn and winter, to allow for weathering, and give the soil time to settle before sowing or planting in spring. Always dig heavy

clay soils then, unless they are wet, and on really heavy clays, it is often better to 'dig' with a fork. Light, sandy soils don't need winter weathering, and since winter weed growth can be a problem on these soils, digging is often best left until spring. Be careful, though; late digging can lead to a puffy, unsettled seed bed, so tread heel-to-toe fashion if in doubt.

Planted-up herbaceous and shrub borders, and bush and cane fruits, benefit from light digging in autumn or early winter. Take care not to damage surface roots. Dig to break in fresh ground, whenever soil and weather conditions are favourable, regardless of the time of year.

When to dig deeply Single digging – digging one-spade deep – turns over the topsoil, and is adequate for most purposes. A lawn will flourish on 10-15cm (4-6in) of well worked soil; 25-30cm (10-12in) suits herbaceous plants, vegetables and dwarf shrubs; trees and large shrubs require a depth of 45cm (18in) or more.

Digging is particularly important in the initial preparations for long-term planting of shrubs, perennials, bush and cane fruits, which occupy the ground for many years. Deep-rooted vegetables like runner beans also need thorough

A mechanical cultivator with a double head makes double digging easier.

soil preparation. For all these plants, it is advisable to double dig, or dig the soil to two spades' depth. Try to double dig a third of the vegetable garden each year. This enables organic matter to be buried deeper and weed roots to be teased out. Double digging is practical only in deep soil. Where a shallow layer of topsoil overlies clay, chalk or limestone, take out planting pockets for trees and shrubs, importing topsoil to work in and around the roots. In the rest of the garden, attempt to increase the soil depth by a little each year.

Sometimes 'hard pans' can be a problem in new building developments, if heavy plant has compacted the subsoil. Double digging is a useful way of breaking this up.

How to dig In the gardening press, various ways of digging are advocated.

Buy a spade which is comfortable and not too heavy to handle. A standard digging spade will get the job done quicker on vacant land than a smaller border spade, but the latter may be easier to use, and is better for digging around border plants. If you have difficulty bending or lifting, try using a spade with spring and lever action.

DOUBLE DIGGING

1. *Double digging and turning the soil into the one before.*

2. *Shovelling in the compost and spreading it evenly.*

3. *Mixing compost in with the broken-up second spit.*

4. *Filling the final trench with soil left over from the first.*

4cm (1½in), invert it in the trench, chop it up and sprinkle with a handful of bonemeal per m (yd) run.

Double digging

Double digging is similar to single, but the bottom of the trench is forked, down to the depth of a spade. Either fork before manuring, or work manure into the lower spit for deep-rooting trees and shrubs. You may find it easier to fork up the bottom if trenches are 60cm (2ft) wide.

Shallow digging

When shallow digging among permanently planted borders, push the spade in obliquely, don't go deeper than 15cm (6in), and be careful of surface roots.

Hints on digging

★ Never bury good topsoil beneath subsoil.

★ Don't try to dig wet soil, or it will puddle and set like concrete when dry.

★ When autumn digging, leave the clods as they fall; the rough surface exposes a greater area to weathering.

★ Use strong footwear, preferably with ankle support.

★ If you are unaccustomed to digging, take a breather after 30 minutes or so.

★ Make sure your spade is clean and sharp. A stainless steel or silvered spade is easier to keep clean than an ordinary steel blade, and ideal if you are likely to do much digging.

★ Clean your spade before putting it away, and wipe over ordinary steel blades with an oily rag to prevent rusting.

Single digging

Starting at one end of the vacant plot, take out a trench 45cm (18in) wide and a spade deep. Set the soil to one side, then skim off the weeds from another 18in (45cm) strip alongside the first, throwing them into the bottom of the first trench. Remove the roots of difficult perennial weeds. Spread a bucket of manure or compost per m (yd) run of trench over the weeds, then dig out a second trench, also a spade deep, inverting the soil and filling in the first trench. Repeat the process, keeping the sides of the trenches vertical, and filling in the last trench from the first.

When breaking in a border from grass, skim the surface off to a depth of

Final ground preparations

Before sowing or planting, break down clods, loosen soil crust, and create a fine tilth. Do this by lightly forking the soil to about 15cm (6in) or by using a powered rotary cultivator. Although forking and rotavating ideally follow digging, they can be used, at a pinch, as

an alternative. If you've been unable to dig, try to go down to at least 25cm (10in) with the fork or rotavator. One drawback is the difficulty of incorporating weeds and manure. Skim off all surface weed with a hoe before forking or rotavating; don't break in fresh grassland with a fork or rotavator. Never fork or rotavate wet ground.

Similar remarks apply to buying a digging fork as to a spade; get one to suit. Buy or hire a powered rotary cultivator that is not too big to manoeuvre in your garden. Unfortunately, rotary cultivators suitable for small gardens are often underpowered, especially if the ground is stony.

Firming and raking The ground may need firming, heel-to-toe fashion, to prevent puffiness, especially after rotary cultivation. Finally, apply fertilizer and rake in, breaking down any soil lumps and creating a level surface.

Compost, manure and fertilisers

Manures are used in large quantities as bulky organic soil conditioners: garden compost, farmyard manure and peat. Their main purpose is to improve and maintain soil texture. Their nutrient content is variable and often regarded as a bonus. Fertilizers are concentrated materials used in relatively small quantities to provide or replenish nutrients.

The value of garden compost When well made, compost is brown, spongy, friable and pleasantly sweet smelling. It contains double or treble the nutrient value of farmyard manure. Compost, for most people, is the cheapest way of providing bulky, organic manure, by recycling garden and household waste.

When compost is used on clay soils, aeration and drainage are improved, 'caking' is reduced and the soil becomes easier to work. Compost increases the moisture retention on light sandy soils, making crops more drought resistant and reducing the excessive loss of nutrients in drainage water, but on these hungry soils, organic matter is soon used up and frequent applications are necessary. Regular compost applications can also help turn the average soil into the ideal.

Composting

The success of composting depends largely on the method. Try to create conditions which encourage the bacteria that play a vital role in the rotting down of vegetable waste. They thrive in warm, airy, non-acid, well drained surroundings.

Use a bin, with a lid to keep out rain. Those bins with slatted wooden sides, about 90cm (3ft) square, are ideal for the average garden. In smaller containers, insufficient heat is generated for bacterial action. Proprietary plastic models of similar capacity also work well. You can improvise, by nailing wire netting to four posts sunk into the ground, and lining the inside with perforated plastic sheet. A free-standing heap is also quite satisfactory, provided it is covered with a heavy-duty plastic sheet weighted down at the corners; 1.2m (4ft) sq is a good size.

In large gardens, have two heaps; build one while the other rots down.

Building a compact heap Start by putting down a 5cm (2in) layer of coarse material like pea or bean haulm, brushwood or stones, to provide aeration and drainage. This is not applicable to those bins with fixed bases. Gradually build up the heap, sandwich fashion, alternating a 15cm (6in) layer of vegetable waste with a scattering of proprietary compost activator, to hasten rotting. Apply another layer of vegetable waste followed by more activator, and repeat until the bin is full. Always keep the bin covered, and

1. *A simple compost container: a square enclosure of 4 strong posts and wire netting.*

2. *A more permanent structure. Spaces within bricks and planks are essential for ventilation.*

3. *A smaller, simpler version of the container shown left. It uses only squared posts and planks.*

lightly water the heap if the contents seem dry. Balance between dry strawy materials and soft waste is important; mix grass clippings with coarser materials to prevent the clippings forming a poultice-like blanket.

★ *Materials to include:* lawn clippings, annual weeds, raw household vegetable trimmings, provided they are neither cooked nor greasy; damp shredded newspaper; pea and bean haulm; soft hedge clippings; and leaves.

★ *Materials to exclude:* seeding weeds; difficult perennial weeds; pest- or disease-infested plants; Brussels sprout stems and woody twigs; chemically treated weeds and lawn clippings; and anything contaminated with creosote.

Rotting down soft materials using activator takes from four to six months in summer, and longer in winter. Turning the heap after about a month can hasten the process, but is not necessary. Compost is ready to use when it has turned brown and crumbly, with an agreeable, earthy smell, and plenty of worm activity.

Other manures As well as compost, the following may prove useful, depending on availability, cost, and your particular soil:

★ *Farmyard manure* is one of the best but difficult to come by. Apply when well rotted; if used fresh is will scorch delicate roots and cause severe mis-shaping if used on root crops.

★ *Mushroom compost* is very good, but the lime content can be high.

★ *Peat* is excellent for improving soil texture, but is expensive, and contains no nutrients.

★ *Straw and bark* are sometimes dug in as manure. Always dress with nitrogenous fertilizer, or bacteria will temporarily rob the soil of nitrogen to sustain themselves as they break down these raw materials.

★ *Branded organic manures* are based on cow, poultry or horse manure, hops and seaweed. Most are available in convenient packs. They are balanced and provide a very useful material, but can be expensive.

★ *Chemical conditioners* If you don't have a ready supply of organic manure, and are battling with heavy clay, chemical conditioners can be invaluable in the short term. They are, however, no substitute for manures and compost.

Manure applications Spreading a layer in the bottom of the trench when digging is traditional. However, it is often better to dig the soil, then fork the manure into the top 23cm (9in) afterwards. The easiest way among established plants is to mulch in spring. Any remaining in autumn is lightly forked in.

Liming

The majority of plants are sensitive to the amount of lime in the soil, whether too much or too little. Lettuce, peas, beetroot and beans yield abysmal crops without lime. Club root disease quickly infects cabbage crops under acid conditions. Clematis, gypsophila, pinks and carnations need lime. Potatoes, tomatoes and celery will tolerate slight acidity, and rhododendrons, azaleas, camellias and heathers soon suffer if subjected to limy soil or hard water.

Lime neutralises soil acidity. (An acid soil restricts the work of beneficial bacteria.) The majority of plant foods are more freely available where there is adequate lime. Lime helps to make heavy soils more crumbly and easily worked, and on light soils lime binds sandy particles together. The calcium supplied in lime is a valuable plant food in its own right.

Initially, the amount of ground limestone to apply can be ascertained by soil testing. An average dressing of lime is a handful of ground limestone per sq m (yd) every third year. Clay soils can be limed more generously than others. Work lime lightly into the soil after digging in winter or spring. Don't apply lime at the same time as fertilizer or manure, or a harmful chemical reaction may result in loss of nutrients. Leave a minimum gap of ten days. In a herbaceous or shrub border, sprinkle lime around plants in winter.

Fertilisers

Nitrogen is needed for leaf and stem growth. Excess produces lush, deep green, soft, disease-prone leaves, at the expense of flowers or fruit. Potash confers hardiness, disease resistance and quality to plants, and balances the effects of nitrogen. Phosphate promotes good root development and encourages plants to flower and fruit earlier.

Small amounts of 'trace' elements are also vital for plant health and well being. Iron, magnesium and boron are examples. Provided the soil is reasonable, and garden compost or manure is used, trace elements rarely present problems. Deficiencies most likely to occur are those of iron and magnesium foliar feeds or soil drenches of iron sequestrene and epsom salts (for the magnesium) usually puts things right.

Types of fertiliser Fertilisers are referred to as 'compound' if they contain a number of nutrients, or 'straight' if they supply only one (these are little used today). There are many proprietary compound mixtures which are economical and easy to use. There is a wide variety for many purposes, and among the specialised fertilisers are those for roses, tomatoes, lawns and chrysanthemums.

Organic fertilisers are natural products, made from plant and animal remains. They usually work out more costly than the inorganics, which are prepared from minerals.

Using fertilisers There are several ways of applying fertilisers, according to the type of plant, time of year, and speed of action desired.

★ *Pre-planting dressings* Slow-acting (base) fertilisers, usually bonemeal (organic) or John Innes base (inorganic), are applied before sowing or planting. For shallow-rooted plants they are lightly raked in when preparing the ground. For trees and shrubs, the fertiliser is worked into the bottom of the planting holes.

★ *Top-dressing* refers to dry fertiliser, normally worked into the top 3cm (1in) of soil. Top-dressing the garden in spring is strongly recommended, using a general fertiliser.

Top-dress with potting compost container plants which are not re-potted annually; scrape away just a bit of the top of the compost and replace it with fresh. Camellias, rhododendrons and magnolias also benefit from a top-dressing of potting compost; the fertiliser in potting compost is diluted, and the peat an added bonus. Lawns, too, respond to a top-dressing of compost in autumn. Top-dress cucumbers and marrows with potting compost, or the shallow feeding surface roots dry out and starve.

★ *Liquid feeding* is generally used to give plants a quick boost in spring and summer. Liquid feeds are short-lived, and repeated applications, often weekly, are needed during flowering or fruiting.

★ *Foliar feeding* gives the most rapid response of all, and is valuable for correcting mineral deficiencies. Special strength proprietary foods are sprayed on to the leaves in dull conditions; never foliar feed in sun, or scorch is likely to follow. Never foliar feed hairy-leaved plants.

★ *Convenience foods* Spikes, pellets and tabs are designed to make feeding easier. Some are suitable for flowering pot plants; for foliage plants; for hanging baskets; windowboxes and containers; for growbags; for acid lovers; or for tomatoes.

A few points to watch The following are common mistakes often made when applying fertilisers.

★ *Don't be overgenerous* Avoid exceeding recommended application rates, or risk root scorch. Even distribution is essential. Avoid overlapping when feeding lawns, and avoid pockets of high concentrations.

★ *Thorough mixing is critical* When making up seed and potting composts, layer the contents up in a heap, and turn at least three times.

★ *Never feed wilting or dry plants* Water them first.

★ *Never use stale fertilisers* They may have undergone a chemical change, and can cause damage.

★ *Do not apply lime with fertilisers or manures* Allow at least a 10-day gap.

PEATY SOIL
Poorly drained; tends to be infertile; too acid for most plants

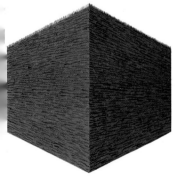

SANDY SOIL
Water drains through very quickly, taking nutrients with it; dries out very quickly in hot weather

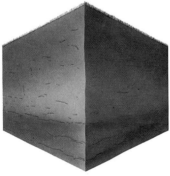

CLAY SOIL
Hard to dig; cold; tends to become waterlogged in winter; cakes hard in hot weather

LOAMY SOIL
The ideal garden soil. All the same, you'll need to do some work to keep it in tip-top condition

● **Drainage** Major work on drainage is best done in autumn. Meanwhile, you can add topsoil for instant results – order it from your local garden centre. Dig two bucketsful into the top 25cm (9in) of each square metre (square yard) of soil

● **Acidity** Improved drainage will help reduce the acidity of the soil. So will liming – sprinkle on 500g (1lb) of hydrated lime per square metre (square yard) every winter

● **Humus** will help sandy soil retain both nutrients and water. Add it by digging in two bucketsful of well-rotted manure or compost per square metre (square yard) every spring or autumn

● **Fertilisers** It's particularly important to keep sandy soils well-supplied with nutrients. Late every spring, sprinkle on a handful of a general fertiliser, such as Growmore, per square metre (square yard) and rake it in lightly. Follow our directions for the additional fertilisers to give individual plants

● **Drainage** Major work on drainage is best done in autumn. Meanwhile, you can help make this heavy soil lighter by sprinkling on hydrated lime in winter. Liming will also make your soil more alkaline, so don't use it if you already have an alkaline soil. If your soil is very acid, you can use up to 500g (1lb) of hydrated lime per square metere (square yard); adjust the quantity according to how acid your soil is.

● **Humus** Humus will also improve the texture. Add it by digging in two bucketsful of well-rotted manure or compost per square metre (square yard) every spring or autumn

● **Drainage** Dig the soil over thoroughly to a depth of at least 25cm (9in) every autumn. Keep the texture perfect by digging in two bucketsful of well-rotted manure or compost per square metre (square yard) every spring and autumn. As long as your soil's not alkaline you can sprinkle on small amounts of hydrated lime in winter – 250g (½lb) per square metre (square yard) should do the trick

Chapter 6

CHOOSING AND GROWING PLANTS

Plants, regardless of type, cannot grow and flourish unless their needs are matched by the prevailing conditions. You need to consider not only their ultimate size and colour, season and nature of interest, but also their soil and site requirements.

To help you make a wise choice, this chapter highlights points to watch when buying and includes lists of plants for 'special purposes'. Whether you are looking for ideas for a small tree as a focal point, shrubs for year-round interest, hardy perennials or bedding plants – you will find a wealth of suggestions. And if you want to try your hand at raising plants from seeds and cuttings, it's all here.

If you are not sure how to go about planting trees, shrubs and hedging, you can pick up practical hints to keep you on the right lines. If roses are for you, look no further for guidelines for their planting, pruning and care.

How to buy plants

The majority of garden plants are known by two names: one botanical and one popular. By international convention, the botanical name is always in Latin. Sometimes the botanical name is also the popular name: clematis, for example, or iris. Some plants have more than one popular name, and sometimes two completely different plants are known by the same name, leading to confusion. However, no plant may have more than one valid Latin name, and this is usually made up of two or three parts. Take thrift as an example: *Armeria maritima* 'Vindictive'.

Armeria is the genus, the surname of a whole group of plants; *maritima* is the species name, which narrows things down to a collection of plants of similar ilk; and, finally, 'Vindictive' is the varietal name which pinpoints one plant only.

When buying plants, always note the whole Latin name, to be sure of getting exactly what you want. This is particularly important in the case of conifers, as the difference between two varieties can be considerable. For

Plants will come in some sort of container. This may be either a rigid pot or soft plastic bag. This protects the root ball and keeps it from breaking up.

example, *Chamaecyparis lawsoniana* 'Albrechti' grows happily to 6m (20ft) while *C.l.* 'Minima Glauca' will not reach 50cm (20in).

Don't be tempted to buy on the spur of the moment, even though colour catalogues and plants seen at garden centres can be very tempting indeed. Consider carefully the needs of the plant, and match them with the conditions you have to offer in your garden; the soil, aspect, sun and shade. Check that the plant is hardy enough to stand the winter, and that it is likely to mature to a suitable size – neither too big nor too small.

Bulbs, corms and tubers Most bulbs, including tulips, hyacinths, crocuses and lilies, are sold by size, measured by the circumference round the middle. Buy bulbs of flowering size, unless you are prepared to wait a year or two for them to grow and develop. Look for firm, healthy, dormant bulbs; avoid any that are soft, or show signs of rotting or premature sprouting.

Bedding plants Avoid tall, weak and spindly plants, or any that are chilled, perhaps displayed outside a shop on a windswept street. Look for short, sturdy plants with healthy foliage of good colour. In the case of bedding and fruiting plants, select those with plenty of bud, but avoid those actually in full flower. These guidelines work equally well for young vegetable plants.

Trees, shrubs and climbers Whether for ornamental or cropping purposes the choice is usually between plants growing in containers or those pre-packed with bare roots.
★ *Container plants* These plants can be set out at almost any time of year provided the soil is moist, but neither watelogged nor frozen. The height of summer and depths of winter are best avoided, in any case. With fruits, stick to the traditional planting times of autumn and early or late winter. If you

CHOOSING PLANTS

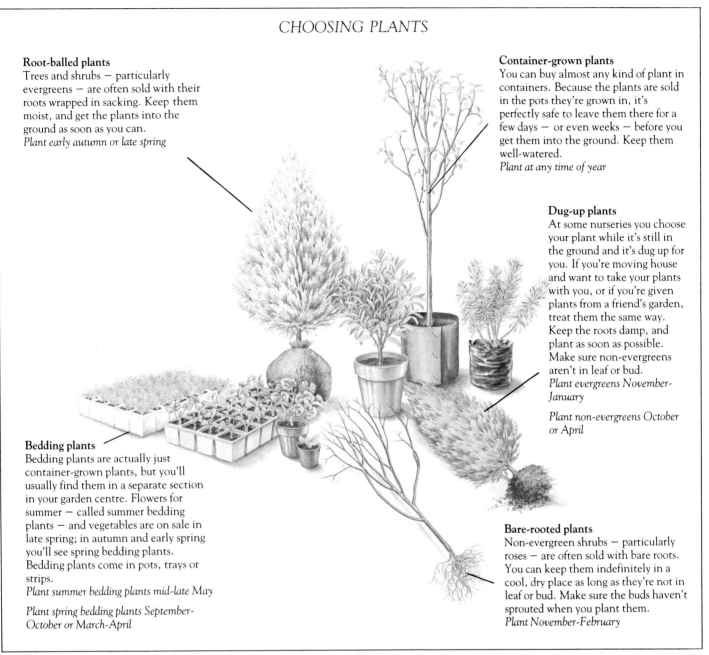

Root-balled plants
Trees and shrubs — particularly evergreens — are often sold with their roots wrapped in sacking. Keep them moist, and get the plants into the ground as soon as you can.
Plant early autumn or late spring

Container-grown plants
You can buy almost any kind of plant in containers. Because the plants are sold in the pots they're grown in, it's perfectly safe to leave them there for a few days — or even weeks — before you get them into the ground. Keep them well-watered.
Plant at any time of year

Dug-up plants
At some nurseries you choose your plant while it's still in the ground and it's dug up for you. If you're moving house and want to take your plants with you, or if you're given plants from a friend's garden, treat them the same way. Keep the roots damp, and plant as soon as possible. Make sure non-evergreens aren't in leaf or bud.
Plant evergreens November-January

Plant non-evergreens October or April

Bedding plants
Bedding plants are actually just container-grown plants, but you'll usually find them in a separate section in your garden centre. Flowers for summer — called summer bedding plants — and vegetables are on sale in late spring; in autumn and early spring you'll see spring bedding plants. Bedding plants come in pots, trays or strips.
Plant summer bedding plants mid-late May

Plant spring bedding plants September-October or March-April

Bare-rooted plants
Non-evergreen shrubs — particularly roses — are often sold with bare roots. You can keep them indefinitely in a cool, dry place as long as they're not in leaf or bud. Make sure the buds haven't sprouted when you plant them.
Plant November-February

want larger plants, choose container-grown specimens. Container-grown plants don't need planting immediately, but the sooner this takes place the better.

Look for sturdy, well rooted plants which are firmly set in their containers. Avoid pot-bound plants with roots growing through the bottom of their containers. Also avoid those with a very large amount of top growth; as a rough guide, the spread of top growth should not be more than twice the container's diameter (climbers excep-

ted). Reject damaged, wilted or dried-out plants; weak spindly growth; and blemished foliage.

Evergreens are best bought in containers; the plants should be well and evenly leafed down to soil level. Once evergreens have gone bare at the base they do not as a rule break out into new growth from old wood. Evergreens 90cm (3ft) high or less are safest; they become established more quickly and easily than larger plants, with less risk of a setback, and very often, after a few years, they overtake the larger plants.

★ *Bare-rooted plants* should be set out in autumn, when dormant. Make sure they have a well developed root system, and be very wary of buying pre-packed plants in plastic bags from hot, centrally heated premises. Any plants which have been standing around for a long time in warm conditions tend to sprout prematurely. They are then weakened, and unlikely to stand up to hard weather after planting. The safest approach to take is to choose freshly delivered plants only, giving you the best chance for a sound, healthy plant.

Planning a mixed border

When gardens were larger, most people has several borders, each devoted to a specific type of plant. There were shrub borders; rose borders; herbaceous perennial borders and bedding-out borders. Each gave a lavish display of colour for part of the year – usually late spring and summer – but were often quite dull the rest of the time. Nowadays, smaller gardens, the high cost of plants, and the fact that hired gardeners are largely a thing of the past, mean that a single border, or perhaps a couple of borders, should contain a glorious mixture of shrubs, perennials, annuals and bulbs, to give colour and interest all year round.

In a small garden, it is better to have fewer borders which can become genuine focal points, than a lot of pocket-handkerchief size beds dotted about the garden, disrupting the flow of a lawn. Remember, wherever lawns abut borders, there is hand-clipping to be done.

Keep to simple-shaped borders, for the same reason, and because they are more attractive than over-fussy, complicated ones, with unnaturally tight curves. If your garden is basically square or rectangular in plan, there is nothing wrong with a straight-edged border; established, well-grown plants will tumble over the edge in any case, breaking up the line and softening any harshness.

If you site your border against a house, wall, fence or hedge, you have an immediate background for the floral display and, in the case of a wall or house, a certain amount of latent heat. With careful siting, all should provide shelter from prevailing winds as well. Making a border along a path is another good idea; you can enjoy the flowers at close range and have reduced maintenance on the path side of the border. Island beds are usually most successful as large-scale plantings, surrounded by a large-scale lawn.

Sun or light shade are equally suitable. There are plants that grow happily in both, and those that quite definitely prefer one or the other. Avoid deep shade, especially from overhanging trees. They will compete with the border plants for nutrients and moisture, as well as blocking out the light, and rain dripping from the leaves is not appreciated by the plants beneath. Avoid windy, exposed positions, which wreak havoc with tall plants and have a drying-out effect.

Try to site the border where it can be seen from the house. The length of the border obviously depends on the size and layout of your garden, but try to make it at least 90cm (3ft) wide. Narrower borders often look mean, and there will be insufficient space for shrubs to mature. Borders over 1.8m (6ft) wide can be difficult to weed and maintain generally, from the edge, and may need a central path of stepping stones.

A mixed border should please the eye with its colours and textures. The plants must be chosen to look interesting not only individually but also as a group.

CHOOSING AND GROWING PLANTS

Perennials for mixed borders

Name	Height	Soil	Site	Features	Season
Acanthus mollis 'Latifolius' Bear's breeches	M	N C	○ ◑	Rose, purple or white flowers; attractive, spiny leaves (C)	Late summer
Achillea 'Moonshine' Yarrow	S	N C	○	Pale-yellow flowers; silvery leaves (C)	Summer
Anemone × hybrida Japanese anemone	S	N C	○ ◑	Pink, red or white flowers	Summer to autumn
Aster Dwarf Hybrids Michaelmas daisy	D-S	A N C	○ ◑	Pink, red, blue or white flowers	Summer to autumn
Astilbe × arendsii vars Spiraea	S	A N C	○ ◑	Pink, red or white flowers (C)	Summer
Coreopsis verticillata Tickseed	S	N C	○	Yellow flowers (C)	Summer to early autumn
Crocosmia masonorum Montbretia	S	A N C	○ ◑	Orange-flame flowers	Summer
Delphinium Belladonna Hybrids Delphinium	M	A N C	○	Blue, white or cream flowers	Summer
Dicentra spectabilis Bleeding Heart	S	A N C	○ ◑	Rose-pink flowers; ferny leaves (C)	Spring to early summer
Digitalis purpurea Hybrids Foxglove	S-M	A N C	◑	Cream, pink and purple flowers (C)	Summer
Echinops humilis vars Globe Thistle	M	N C	○	Steel-blue flowers	Summer
Erigeron named vars Fleabane	S	A N C	○	Blue or pink flowers (C)	Summer
Geum 'Mrs Bradshaw' Avens	S	A N C	○ ◑	Crimson-red flowers (C)	Spring to autumn

Key to heights: D = Dwarf; 30cm (12in) or less   S = Small; 30-90cm (12-36in)   M = Medium; 90-150cm (3-5ft)
T = Tall; over 1.5m (5ft)   (C) = Can be grown in containers

Coreopsis verticillata

Erigeron

Dicentra spectabilis

Perennials for mixed borders (continued)

Name	Height	Soil	Site	Features	Season
Helenium named vars Helenium	M	A N C	○	Bronze, crimson or gold flowers	Summer
Helleborus niger Christmas rose	D-S	N	○ ◐	White flowers; evergreen leaves (C)	Winter to spring
Hemerocallis named vars Day lily	S-M	A N C	○ ◐	Gold, pink, purple, red or orange flowers (C)	Summer
Hosta fortunei Plaintain lily	S	A N C	◐ ●	Lilac-mauve flowers; broad variegated leaves (C)	Summer to autumn
Iris germanica vars Bearded iris	M	N C	○ ◐	Blue, pink, red, yellow, white or maroon flowers	Spring and early summer
Kniphofia galpinii Hybrids Red hot poker	S	N	○ ◐	Cream, gold, orange, red or bicoloured flowers (C)	Summer to autumn
Nepeta × faassenii Catmint	D-S	N C	○	Lavender-mauve flowers; aromatic grey foliage (C)	Spring to autumn
Paeonia officinalis vars Peony	S	A N C	○	Crimson, pink or white scented flowers	Spring and summer
Phlox paniculata Border phlox	S-M	A N C	○ ◐	Scented pink, purple, red, white or bicoloured flowers (C)	Summer to autumn
Primula japonica Japanese primula	S	A N	◐	Purple-red flowers (C)	Spring to early summer
Sedum spectabile vars Stonecrop	S	A N C	○	Magenta-rose flowers (C)	Late summer and autumn
Solidago Mimosa	T	A N C	○ ◐	Golden yellow flowers	Summer to early autumn
Golden Thumb, Golden Rod	D-S	A N C	○ ◐	Clear yellow flowers (C)	Summer

Key to heights: D = Dwarf; 30cm (12in) or less   S = Small; 30-90cm (12-36in)   M = Medium; 90-150cm (3-5ft)
T = Tall; over 1.5m (5ft)   (C) = Can be grown in containers

Kniphofia galpinii

Nepeta × faassenii

Sedum spectabile

Summer bedding plants from seed

Name	Sow	Temp.	Method	Prick out into
Ageratum Floss flower	February-March	A	Surface sow	Trays or singly into small pots
Alyssum Sweet alyssum	Early March	C	Cover	Trays
Antirrhinum Snapdragon	February	W	Surface sow	Trays
Begonia Fibrous and tuberous rooted	December-February	W	Surface sow	Singly into small pots
Calceolaria rugosa Slipper flower	January-February	A	Surface sow	Trays, then singly into small pots
Callistephus China/annual aster	March	A	Cover	Trays
Dahlia Bedding dahlias	February-March	A	Cover	Singly into small pots
Gazania	February-March	W	Cover	Singly into small pots
Heliotropium Cherry pie	February	W	Surface sow	Singly into small pots
Impatiens Busy lizzie	February-March	W	Surface sow	Singly into small pots
Kochia Burning bush	March	C	Cover	Singly into small pots
Lobelia	February	W	Surface sow	Into trays, in clumps of three or more
Matthiola Stocks	March	C	Cover	Trays or singly into small pots

Key to temperature requirements: C = 13-16°C (55-60°F) Cool (windowsill)   A = 16-18°C (60-65°F) Average (windowsill)
W = 18-21°C (65-70°F) Warm (best germinated in a propagator)

Begonia

Lobelia

Gazania

Summer bedding plants from seed (continued)

Name	Sow	Temp.	Method	Prick out into
Mesembryanthemum Ice plant	February-March	A	Cover	Trays or singly into small pots
Nicotiana Tobacco plant	February-March	W	Surface sow	Trays or singly into small pots
Pelargonium Bedding geranium	January-February	W	Cover	Singly into small pots
Petunia	February	W	Surface sow	Trays or singly into small pots
Rudbeckia (annual vars) Cone flower	February-March	A	Cover	Trays
Salvia Scarlet sage	February	W+	Cover	Singly into small pots
Tagetes French marigold	February-March	A	Cover	Trays
Thunbergia Black-eyed Susan	March	W	Cover	Singly into small pots
Tropaeolum Nasturtium	March-April	C	Cover	Singly into small pots
Verbena Vervain	February	W	Cover	Singly into small pots
Viola Pansy & viola	February-March	C	Cover	Trays or singly into small pots

Key to temperature requirements: C = 13-16°C (55-60°F) Cool (windowsill)   A = 16-18°C (60-65°F) Average (windowsill)
W = 18-21°C (65-70°F) Warm (best germinated in a propagator)

Petunia

Tagetes

Viola

Hardy bulbs, corms and tubers for mixed borders

Name	Height	Site	Soil	Nature/season of interest
Agapanthus 'Headbourne Hybrids' African lily	60-90cm (2-3ft)	○	A N C	Blue flowers in late summer and early autumn.
Chionodoxa luciliae Glory of the snow	8-15cm (3-6in)	○ ◑	A N C	Starry blue flowers in early spring.
Crocus *chrysanthus* vars	8cm (3in)	○ ◑	A N C	Yellow, white, blue or bronze flowers in late winter.
speciosus vars	10-13cm) (4-5in)			White or blue flowers in autumn and early winter.
tomasinianus vars	8cm (3in)	○ ◑	A N C	Lavender or purple flowers in late winter.
Endymion non-scriptus Bluebell	20-30cm (8-12in)	○ ◑	A N	Violet-blue flowers in spring.
Fritillaria imperialis Crown imperial	60-90cm (24-36in)	○ ◑	A N C	Orange, yellow or red flowers in spring.
Galanthus nivalis Snowdrop	20cm (8in)	◑	A N C	White flowers in winter.
Iris *reticulata*	15cm (6in)	○	C	Blue-violet flowers in winter.
danfordiae	13cm (5in)	○	C	Yellow flowers in winter.
English, Dutch and Spanish	60cm (24in)	○	N C	Blue, white, purple, pink, yellow or bronze flowers in summer.

Agapanthus

Crocus chrysanthus

Iris reticulata

Hardy bulbs, corms and tubers for mixed borders

Name	Height	Site	Soil	Nature/season of interest
Lilium				
candidum (Madonna lily)	120cm (4ft)	○ ◑	N C	White trumpet flowers in summer.
martagon (Turk's cap lily)	90-150cm (3-5ft)	○	A N C	Pink, purple or wine-red flowers in summer; many hybrids available.
Oriental hybrids	90-190cm (3-6ft)	○	A N C	Spotted, bicoloured flowers in crimson, white, pink, salmon, maroon or vermilion in summer.
Mid-Century hybrids	60cm (24in)	○ ◑	A N	Yellow, orange, crimson, red, pink, maroon or bicoloured flowers in summer.
Muscari armeniacum Grape hyacinth	25cm (10in)	○	A N C	Blue flowers in mid-spring.
Narcissus various Daffodil	8-45cm (3-18in)	○ ◑	A N C	Yellow, gold, orange, white or bicoloured flowers in spring.
Nerine bowdenii	60cm (24in)	○	A N C	Pink flowers in autumn.
Ornithogalum umbellatum Star of Bethlehem	20-30cm (8-12in)	○ ◑	A N C	White flowers in late spring.
Schizostylis coccinea Kaffir lily	30cm (12in)	○	A N C	Crimson flowers in late autumn.
Scilla tubergeniana	8-10cm (3-4in)	○ ◑	A N C	Pale-blue flowers in late winter and early spring.
Tulipa various Tulip	10-75cm (4-30in)	○	A N C	Pink, red, white, gold, orange or bicoloured flowers.

Lilium candidum

Muscari armeniacum

Nerine bowdenii

Permanent and temporary plants
Shrubs, trees and climbers are a long-term investment in labour-saving gardening, but they often take a year or two, sometimes longer, to make a visual impact. Annuals provide the quickest show, but they only last a season. When planning your mixed border, concentrate on getting the long-term plants right, and spaced well enough apart to give them room to grow. (Most garden centres label plants, or groups of plants, to indicate their expected mature size. If in doubt, ask.) Site tall-growing plants at the back of a one-sided border; in an island bed, place them in the middle.

Newly planted shrubs look disappointing, surrounded by vast expanses of bare soil for several years. Still, it is important to stick to the recommended spacing; crowding shrubs together only results in wastage, as some will need removing once growth gets underway. Another alternative is to buy reasonably mature shrubs, but this works out very expensive, and large shrubs are slower to become established than smaller ones. The best alternative is to interplant the young shrub with temporary fillers. These may be perennials, bulbs, bedding plants or even quick-growing, inexpensive shrubs. As the permanent plants grow, temporary plants are reduced in number, though a mixed border should always have some room for these delightful, temporary displays. Annuals, perennials and bulbs tend to look nicer when planted in informal groups or drifts, rather than in straight lines.

It is important never to allow filler plants to block out light, touch permanent plants, or compete seriously with them for available moisture and nutrients.

Time-scales Summer bedding plants give almost instant return for money; planted out in May or June, they come into flower within the month, and give colour until the first autumn frosts.

Petunias, marigolds, and salvias are popular annuals. Autumn-planted spring-flowering bulbs, like tulips and daffodils, along with biennials like forget-me-nots and wallflowers, come into bloom about six months after planting, and last for several weeks. The biennials are then discarded, while the crocus, daffodils and narcissi can be left to naturalise and will bloom each spring for many years. Tulips are slightly different; they need to be lifted in summer, dried off, and re-planted in autumn. Again, they will last for many years.

Perennials, such as hostas, day lilies, golden rod and Michaelmas daisies, are planted in autumn or spring and will put on a show within twelve months of planting. Most continue to flower year after year, but they tend to become overcrowded, and usually need lifting and dividing every four to five years.

A garden that is visually exciting; here shown in late spring.

Evergreen Shrubs

Name	Size	Soil	Site	Features/season of interest
A. *Aucuba japonica* 'Variegata' Aucuba/Spotted laurel	M	A N C	○ ◑ ●	Large, glossy gold-spotted leaves; berries on female plants in autumn.
B. *Berberis darwinii* Barberry	M	A N C	○ ◑	Orange-gold flowers in spring; blue-purple berries in summer; small, shiny dark leaves
C. *Camellia japonica* vars Camellia	M/T	A	○ ◑	White, pink, red or bicoloured spring flowers; large, glossy leaves.
D. *Ceanothus dentatus* Californian lilac	M	N C	○	Powder-blue flowers in early summer; small shiny leaves
E. *Choisya ternata* Mexican orange	M	A N	○ ◑ ●	Scented white flowers in spring and summer; large, glossy, aromatic leaves.
F. *Cotoneaster conspicuus*	M	A N C	○ ◑	White flowers in summer; red berries in autumn;
G. *conspicuus* 'Decorus' Cotoneaster	D	A N C	○ ◑	dark-green leaves with grey undersides.
H. *Elaeagnus pungens* 'Maculata' Elaeagnus	M	N C	○ ◑	Large, shiny, golden, variegated leaves.
I. *Euonymus fortunei* vars Winter creeper	P/S	N C	○ ◑ ●	Glossy green or variegated leaves; self-clinging if grown against walls.
J. *Hebe* 'Autumn Glory' Shrubby veronica	S	N C	○	Violet-blue flowers in summer/early autumn; glossy green leaves.
K. *Hypericum calycinum* Rose of Sharon	D	A N C	○ ◑	Golden flowers in summer; long, bright-green leaves.
L. *Ilex aquifoium* vars Holly	M/T	A N C	○ ◑ ●	Red berries on female plants in winter; shiny green or variegated leaves.
M. *Lavandula spica* Lavender	D/S	N C	○	Blue, lavender or purple flowers; grey or silvery green aromatic leaves.

Cotoneaster conspicuus

Ceanothus dentatus

Hypericum calycinum

Evergreen Shrubs

Name	Size	Soil	Site	Features/season of interest
N. *Mahonia aquifolium* Oregon grape	S	A N C	◑ ●	Fragrant gold flowers in spring; blue-black berries in summer; large shiny green leaves.
O. *Olearia × haastii* Daisy bush	M	N C	○	Scented white flowers in summer; grey-green leaves.
P. *Pernettya mucronata* Pernettya	D	A	◑ ●	Pink, red or white berries autumn to spring; small glossy leaves.
Q. *Pieris floribunda* Andromeda	M	A N	◑	White, lily-of-the-valley flowers in spring; glossy green leaves
R. *Pyracantha rogersiana* Firethorn	M/T	A N C	○ ◑	White flowers in summer; red or gold berries in autumn and winter; glossy, lance-shaped leaves.
S. *Rhododendron* hybrids Azaleas and rhododendrons	D/T	A	○ ◑	Pink, red, gold, orange and white flowers in spring; dark-green leaves.
T. *Rosmarinus officinalis* Rosemary	M	N C	○	Blue flowers in spring; aromatic grey-green leaves.
U. *Senecio* 'Sunshine' Senecio	S	N C	○ ◑	Silvery grey-green leaves with white undersides; gold flowers in summer.
V. *Viburnum davidii* Viburnum	S	N C	◑ ●	White summer flowers; blue berries on female plants in autumn; large glossy ribbed leaves.

Key to heights: P = Prostrate or creeping habit   D = Dwarf; 30-75cm (12-30in)   S = Small; 75cm-1.5m (30in-5ft)

M = Medium; 1.5-3m (5-10ft)   T = Tall; over 3m (10ft)

Shrubs for special purposes:

Shrubs for ground cover
A, F, G, I, J, K, M, N, P, S, T, U, V

Shrubs for town gardens
A, B, C, D, E, F, G, H, I, J, K, L, M, N, P, Q, R, S, T, U, V

Shrubs for coastal areas
A, B, D, F, H, I, J, K, L, M, N, O, R, T, U, V

Pyracantha rogersiana

Rhododendron

Viburnum davidii

Deciduous Shrubs

Name	Size	Soil	Site	Features/season of interest
A. *Berberis thunbergii* vars Barberry	S	A N C	○ ◑	Gold spring flowers; red or green foliage; red berries and brilliant foliage in autumn.
B. *Buddleia davidii* vars Butterfly bush	M/T	N C	○	Fragrant pink, purple, red or white flowers in summer.
C. *Caryopteris × Clandeonensis* Blue spiraea	S	N C	○	Blue flowers in late summer; aromatic grey-green leaves.
D. *Ceratostigma willmorttianum* Hardy plumbago	D/S	N C	○	Blue flowers in late summer; green leaves turning red in autumn.
E. *Cornus alba* 'Sibirica' Dogwood	M	A N C	◑	Brilliant crimson stems in winter; green summer foliage turning red in autumn.
F. *Cotoneaster horizontalis* Fishbone cotoneaster	P	A N C	○ ●	White flowers in summer; red berries and foliage in autumn.
G. *Cytisus scoparius* vars Broom	M	A N C	○	Gold, maroon, pink or red flowers in summer.
H. *Escallonia* named varieties Escallonia	M	N C	○ ◑	Pink, red or white summer flowers; small glossy leaves; some forms semi-evergreen.
I. *Forsythia intermedia* Golden bell bush	M	A N C	○ ◑	Golden spring flowers; green leaves.
J. *Fuchsia magellanica* vars Fuchsia	S/M	A N C	○ ◑	Pink, red or white flowers in summer; green leaves.
K. *Hamamelis × intermedia* vars Witch hazel	M	A	○ ◑	Gold flowers in winter; green leaves turning gold in autumn.
L. *Hydrangea macrophylla* vars Hydrangea	S/M	A N C	○ ◑	Blue, pink or white flowers in summer.
M. *Ligustrum ovalifolium* 'Aureum' Golden privet	M	A N C	○ ◑	Golden variegated leaves.

Cornus alba 'Sibirica'

Ligustrum ovalifolium 'Aureum'

Forsythia intermedia

Deciduous Shrubs

Name	Size	Soil	Site	Features/season of interest
N. *Philadelphus* 'Sybille'	S	N C	◯ ◑	Scented white flowers in summer; green leaves.
O. *Potentilla fruticosa* vars Shrubby cinquefoil	D/S	A N C	◯	Gold, cream, tangerine, or white flowers in summer; small green leaves.
P. *Prunus triloba* Flowering almond	M	N C	◯	Pink spring flowers; mid-green, toothed leaves.
Q. *Ribes sanguineum* Flowering currant	M	A N C	◯ ◑	Pink or red flowers in spring; blue berries in summer; green leaves.
R. *Rosa* species vars Rose	S/M	A N C	◯	Pink, purple, red or white scented flowers in summer.
S. *Sambucus nigra* 'Aurea' Golden elder	M/T	A N C	◯ ◑	Golden foliage; white flowers in summer followed by black berries.
T. *Spiraea* x *bumalda* vars Spiraea	D/S	A N C	◯ ◑	Carmine flowers in summer; variegated pink and green, or gold and green foliage.
U. *Symphoricarpos* x *doorenbosii* vars Snowberry	S/M	A N C	◯ ◑	Carmine, pink or white berries in autumn; green leaves.
V. *Viburnum carlesii* Viburnum	S/M	N C	◯	Pink buds opening to scented white flowers in spring; autumn foliage tints.
W. *Weigela* hybrids Weigela	M	A N C	◯ ◑	Pink or red flowers in early summer; green or variegated leaves.

Key as for evergreens.

Shrubs for special purposes:

Shrubs for ground cover
A, D, F, G, J, O, R, T, U, V

Shrubs for town gardens
A, B, D, E, F, G, I, J, K, M, N, O, P, Q, P, S, T, U, V, W

Shrubs for coastal areas
A, B, C, D, E, F, G, H, I, J, L, M, O, P, Q, R, S, T, V, W

Potentilla fruticosa

Rosa

Ribes sanguineum

Trees for small gardens

Practical considerations When choosing trees, especially for small gardens, consider their size in ten or twenty years' time. Trees which outgrow their space usually outgrow their welcome, and tend to be cut down, or butchered back to size. This is a pity when there are many suitable candidates for small gardens.

Tree roots can affect building foundations, which can be damaged directly by roots forcing their way into small cracks and eventually enlarging them. Tree roots take in copious amounts of water, drying out the soil under foundations. This can result in soil shrinkage, especially on heavy clay soils, uneven settlement of the building, and consequent cracking of walls. Certain trees – willows, poplars and major forest trees – are notorious for the damage

caused by their roots, and should be kept well away from buildings. For similar reasons, these trees should be kept away from drains. Trees planted up against a house can block out light and fill drains and gutters with falling leaves each autumn. Some trees – birch, for example – have relatively sparse, light foliage and are less troublesome in this respect.

Finally, as with any other plant, be sure to match the needs of your tree with the prevailing site and soil conditions in your garden.

Design considerations In small gardens, trees are usually planted as single specimens, perhaps to provide a focal point in a lawn or shrub border. Occasionally, if space allows they are planted in clumps, or for screening. Colourful flowers and foliage are important, and the red and gold autumn tints of some varieties of thorn, birch and maple are

Trees should be carefully chosen for size, colour and texture. This garden is a careful blend and is especially beautiful in the autumn as shown.

quite outsanding. Don't, however overlook trees with eye-catching berries or fruits, or colourful stems. Try t choose 'double bonus trees': the plum leaf-thorn (*Crataegus prunifolia*), fo instance, has white, scented flowers i summer, red autumn berries and yellow and crimson autumn foliage.

Consider, too, tree shape. Weepin trees make splendid lawn specimens narrow pyramidal or columnar trees ar ideal where space is restricted. Round oval, or wide-spreading trees, dense open texture, are all variations to con sider. The shape of deciduous trees particularly important. Their leafle form is visible for half the year, an those with graceful growth habit ar double value for the space they occupy

Hardy trees for small gardens

Name	Ht × Sp	Light	Nature/season of interest
A. *Acer palmatum* Japanese Maple	4.5×3.5m (15×12ft)	○ ◑	Rounded, oval shape; red or green leaves turning red, yellow, orange in autumn. Deciduous.
B. *pseudoplatanus* 'Brilliantissimum' Sycamore	4.5×4.5m (15×15ft)	○ ◑	Mop-headed; young leaves pink, turning green in summer. Deciduous.
C. *Alnus incana* 'Aurea' Alder	4.5×2.5m (15×8ft)	○	Conical; young shoots and leaves gold; yellow spring catkins; orange bark. Deciduous.
D. *Betula pendula* 'Youngii' Weeping Birch	4×4m (13×13ft)	○ ◑	Weeping; green leaves turning yellow in autumn; bark silvery. Deciduous.
E. *pendula* 'Fastigiata' Silver Birch	5×3m (17×10ft)	○ ◑	Pyramidal, narrow, upright; green leaves turning gold in autumn. Deciduous.
F. *Cotoneaster hybridus* 'Pendulus' Weeping Cotoneaster	3×3m (10×10ft)	○ ◑	Weeping; white flowers in summer; red berries autumn/winter. Semi-evergreen.
G. *Crataegus prunifolia* Plum-leaf thorn	5×4m (17×13ft)	○	Rounded; white summer flowers; red winter fruits; green leaves turning red and orange in autumn. Deciduous.
H. *Ilex aquifolium* Holly	5×3m (17×10ft)	○ ◑	Conical; shiny green or variegated leaves; red winter berries. Evergreen
I. *Laburnum × watereii vossii* Laburnum	5×4m (17×13ft)	○ ◑	Rounded; pendulous racemes of gold flowers May/June. Deciduous.
J. *Malus sargentii* Crab apple	3×3m (10×10ft)	○	Rounded, wide spreading; white spring flowers followed by small red apples in summer. Deciduous.
K. *Prunus cerasifera* 'Nigra' Purple-leaved Plum	6×4m (20×13ft)	○ ◑	Rounded; pink spring flowers; leaves deep-wine to purple brown. Deciduous.
L. *serrulata* 'Erecta' Lombardy poplar cherry	5×0.6m (17×2ft)	○	Narrow, columnar; pink flowers in spring.
M. *serrulata* 'Kanzan' Japanese cherry	6×4m (20×13ft)	○	Vase-like crown; pink spring flowers; bronzy leaves turning green in summer, then red in autumn.
N. *Pyrus salicifolia* 'Pendula' Weeping pear	4×4m (13×13ft)	○ ◑	Weeping; creamy-white flowers in spring; grey leaves. Deciduous.
O. *Salix purpurea* 'Pendula' Weeping willow	5×4m (17×13ft)	○ ◑	Weeping; purple bark; green leaves. Deciduous.
P. *Sorbus aucuparia* Mountain ash	6×5m (20×17ft)	○ ◑	Oval headed; white flowers in early summer followed by red berries. Deciduous.
Q. *aria × hostii* Whitebeam	4×3m (13×10ft)	○	Rounded; grey leaves; pink flowers in May; red berries and leaf tints in autumn. Deciduous.

Trees for special purposes:

Trees for acid soil
A, B, C, D, E, F, H, I, J, K, N, O, P, Q

Flowering trees
C, F, G, I, J, K, L, M, N, P, Q

Trees for autumn leaf tints
A, D, E, G, M, P, Q

Trees for neutral and chalky soil
B, C, D, E, F, G, H, I, J, K, L, M, N, O

Berrying and fruiting trees
F, G, H, J, P, Q

Trees for towns
B, C, D, E, F, G, H, I, J, K, L, M, N, O, P, Q

Know your roses

Use this page to check what types of roses you have in your garden – then follow our guidelines for when and how to prune them. The text on the next page applies to unpruned roses. If you've just taken over a garden in which the roses have already been pruned – all you'll see is just a few short stumps – it's best to play safe and leave them alone until they've flowered, and then consult this page to work out what they are.

Standard Rose bushes grafted on to single stems about 1m ($3\frac{1}{8}$ft) high. Popular varieties: City of Belfast, Fragrant Cloud, Iceberg, King's Ransom, Super Star.

Weeping standard Long, trailing branches grafted on to 1.2-1.8m (4-6ft) stems. Popular varieties: Albertine, Canary Bird, Crimson Shower, Emily Gray, Excelsior.

Floribundas Flowers carried in clusters; tend to be smaller than those of hybrid tea roses, and not as well formed, but much more plentiful. Long flowering season. Popular varieties: Allgold, Arthur Bell, Baby Bio, Orange Sensation, Queen Elizabeth.

Miniature bush Range in height from 15cm (6in) to 45cm (18in); flowers no more than 5cm (2in) across. Popular varieties: Baby Masquerade, Darling Flame, Pour Toi, Scarlet Gem, Starina, Yellow Doll.

Hybrid tea Large, well-shaped blooms, carried one to a stem or in small groups. Flower in flushes throughout the summer. Popular varieties: Alec's Red, Peace, Prima Ballerina, Silver Jubilee, Wendy Cussons, Whisky Mac.

Shrub Vast range of bushy roses: most are large, many have arching branches, some are grown for their attractive leaves and fruits as well as for their flowers. Flowering season tends to be short with old varieties. Shrub roses include wild roses and their close relatives (called 'species' roses), 'old fashioned' roses (most of them bred before 1900) and 'modern shrub' roses (mainly bred from species and old roses). Popular varieties include such names as: Canary Bird, Cecile Brunner, Fred Loads, Golden Wings, Nevada, *Rosa rubrifolia* (species).

Climber or rambler Long, flexible branches needing support; flowers carried one to a stem or in clusters. Flowering season tends to be short. Popular varieties: Albertine, Casino, Danse du Feu (long flowering), Dorothy Perkins, Golden Showers, Mermaid, Pink Perpetue.

Rosa Dorothy Perkins

Rosa Albertine

Rosa Super Star

Rosa Pink Perpetue

Rosa Mermaid

Rosa Peace

Get your roses into shape

If you want to get the best out of your roses, you're going to have to prune them – it's as simple as that. Pruning's easy – don't let anyone tell you it isn't. All you have to do is find the technique that's best suited to your particular plants. Here's an easy-to-follow guide to the roses in your garden, with features on the best and simplest ways of pruning them – and how and when to do it.

Why prune? Each branch of a rose plant will flower for only so long. Every spring new shoots begin to form, and the plant puts most of its energy into growing them. It's the old wood that suffers – it's gradually starved, its flowers decrease in both quantity and quality until it finally stops producing them altogether, and eventually it dies. So, as far as flowers are concerned, there comes a point when old wood is nothing but a burden to the plant: it's better off without it. The main reason for pruning is to remove worn-out old branches whose flowering days are all but over, and to let the plant put all its strength into producing vigorous young shoots that will bear lots of perfect blooms.

There's another important reason for pruning. Left to themselves, roses tend to sprawl; by clever pruning, you can encourage them to keep a compact and well-balanced shape, which will be an asset to your garden.

When should you prune? Although it's possible to prune roses at any time from late autumn to spring without doing serious harm to the plant, you'll find it's generally most convenient to do it in the spring. For one thing, it's easier to see what you're doing when there are no leaves on the plant. And it's also better for the plant: pruning tends to stimulate new growth, and if you prune in the autumn or winter, you may be

A simple routine of regular pruning is all it takes to ensure you have a stunning show of perfectly formed roses year after year.

running the risk of frosty weather damaging tender young shoots.

Unfortunately, however, there's a little bit more to it than that. With most roses it's the new shoots that carry the summer's best flowers, so it's perfectly safe to cut away old wood in the spring – you can be sure it wouldn't have carried the best flowers in any case. But there are some roses whose shoots don't start producing blooms until they're a year old – so if you cut out

old wood in the spring, you may be doing yourself out of some flowers! It makes sense, with these, to leave pruning until autumn, when the flowering season's over.

It's also a good idea to prune tall roses in the autumn – they're easily damaged by high winds and rain, so you should cut them back before the really bad weather starts.

How can you tell when it's best to prune _your_ roses? Only by knowing what kind they are. Read the descriptions on p. 82 to find out what kinds of roses you have in your garden, and when to prune them for the best results.

Pruning roses

The object of pruning is to cut away old and dead wood so that the plant can concentrate its energies on new, productive growth. The guidelines here apply to pruning all types of roses.

It's important to use sharp secateurs to ensure that you cut the stem cleanly. If the stem is crushed or bruised, it may die, and you will have wasted your time.

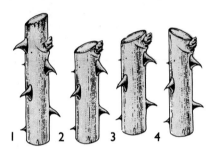

Cut not more than 6mm (¼in) above a new bud. If you cut any higher (1), you will leave a stub that will eventually rot and provide ideal conditions for disease, which may infect the whole plant. On the other hand, cutting too close to the bud (2) is likely to damage it. Angle the cut so that it slopes gently away from the bud (3). If you cut in the wrong direction (4), moisture is likely to collect near the bud and cause it to rot.

Make your pruning cuts just above outward facing buds. This will mean that the new shoots will grow away from the centre of the plant, resulting in a well-balanced, open shape.

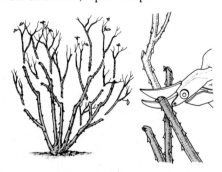

With roses that tend to sprawl, it's worth pruning some branches which appear above inward facing buds. This will encourage the plant to grow into a more compact shape which is also more attractive.

If two or three shoots develop from one bud after pruning, remove all but the strongest by pinching them out with your fingers.

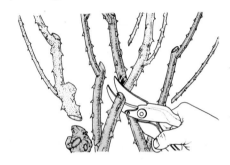

Cut back dead or diseased wood to just above a healthy bud: check that the cut surface is white, not brown or grey. All weak or very thin stems should be pruned severely to encourage more robust growth: cut them back to the point where they meet strong stems, or to ground level. If two branches rub, shorten the thinner branch to a bud below the point where they cross.

Removing suckers Most roses are made up of two different plants: the best flowering varieties are grafted on to those with good, strong root systems. Occasionally, the root system, which is known as the root stock, produces a stem of its own – a sucker. This uses energy that would otherwise go to the flowering part – called the scion – so you should remove it immediately. Suckers are fairly easy to identify: they're whip-like stems, often thornier than branches of the scion, and they rarely bear flowers; if they do, the blooms will look quite different from those on the rest of the plant. Suckers join the plant at the root, so it is possible that you may need to clear away some soil so that you can trace them back to the plant.

Cut or wrench the suckers off at the point they grow from; if you cut them off at ground level, you'll only encourage any buds on the part of the sucker that's left below ground to sprout and make new suckers.

Pruning hybrid teas, floribundas and miniatures

Hybrid teas Any time between mid-February and late March cut out any dead or diseased wood and thin stems, then shorten the thickest shoots to 20cm (8in), the thinner ones to 15cm (6in). By June or July new shoots will have grown, and it is on these that the season's flowers will grow.

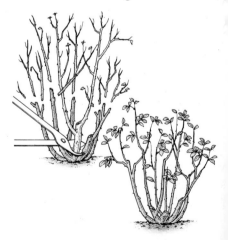

Remove faded blooms throughout the flowering season by cutting the stem back to the first young shoot below the flower (this process is known as dead

heading and it encourages the production of more flowers, keeping your garden colourful throughout the whole season).

When planting bare-rooted hybrid teas, remove dead wood and trim long or damaged roots, then cut off the tips of the main stems just above the highest bud. In February or March, trim each shoot to about 15cm (6in). When planting those grown in containers, simply cut out dead or damaged wood, leaving all other pruning until the following spring.

Floribundas Treat floribundas in much the same way as hybrid teas, but don't cut them back as much. Each spring, remove dead or diseased wood and cut out very thin stems, then shorten all stems by about a quarter of their length. New shoots will form by early summer, to bear the season's flowers.

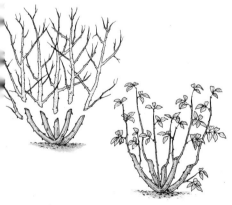

As the flowers fade, remove the whole cluster, or truss, by cutting the stem back to the first strong outward pointing shoot below it.

When planting floribundas, trim long or damaged roots and remove dead wood. Do nothing more to container-grown plants until the following spring. With bare-rooted types, however, trim the main branches; then, in February or March, shorten all shoots to about 23cm (9in).

Miniature bushes Prune miniature roses in the spring by cutting out thin or dead stems and shortening the remaining branches by about a third of their length. Remove dead flowers throughout the summer by cutting below the flower cluster, as with floribundas.

Miniatures need only light pruning before planting: simply trim the roots, and any long branches. In February or March cut back strong shoots to about 15cm (6in) and cut out weak or dead wood.

Pruning new roses It's a good idea to prune new roses just after you plant them. By cutting out old, weak and diseased wood, you can help the plant settle down and put its energy into growing healthily, so that it will develop strong roots and a sound framework of sturdy branches. After this initial pruning it's best to leave the plant alone for a while: you should prune it again the following spring or autumn, depending on the type. Some suppliers sell rose plants ready pruned, so when you're buying your roses you should ask when you next need to prune them, or consult the instructions on the packaging.

Albertine, a rambling rose, drapes well over a boundary wall (right).

Pruning climbing and rambling roses

Initial pruning Prune roses immediately after planting, usually between autumn and spring, to encourage strong new growth and flowering wood. Cut the main stems back to a good bud, about 50cm (20in) above ground. After pruning, tie in the main stems at an oblique angle of 40-50°. This encourages even branching from soil level upwards. Prune other weaker basal growths back to about 10cm (4in).

Routine pruning Both climbers and ramblers are pruned in autumn after flowering. With climbers, encourage the formation of a permanent framework of main stems, which are retained for a number of years. Branches grow from this framework and it is these branchlets which carry the flowers. Deadhead regularly during the growing season. After flowering, cut the flowered branches back to within a bud of the main framework.

Many ramblers differ from climbers in that the flowers are produced along the length of stems formed the previous year. Ramblers' natural habit of producing vigorous new stems from the base makes pruning quite simple. After flowering, cut out spent flowered stems nearly back to soil level and tie in the strongest new growths as replacements. Cut out any surplus to requirements.

Roses are sold either in containers or with their roots completely bare. Treat container-grown plants just as you would established ones; you'll need to prune bare-rooted plants a little harder in their first year to get the best results.

Renovating roses If the roses in your garden have been left unpruned for a number of years, they'll probably look a terrible mess: a tangle of dead and dying branches that carry only a very few flowers, probably harbouring all sorts of unpleasant diseases. If you have a rose like this, resist the temptation to dig it up and put something else in its place. Luckily, roses respond very well to ruthless pruning, and it's easy to make them bloom like new again.

You'll need to cut the plant back severely. Some roses can be cut down all at once, but others won't survive such drastic treatment. So we'd advise you to spread the work over two years, tackling half the plant at a time. You should start renovating a rose at the time of year that's best for pruning it – look at the flow chart to find out when to begin work on the roses you've got.

Renovating bush roses

You may feel rather alarmed at the idea of lopping whole branches off a bush rose, but it's really the only way to make an overgrown plant strong and healthy again so that it can produce lots of flowers. If the bush has been neglected for a long time, some of the branches may be too thick to be cut cleanly with secateurs; if you have any difficulties, use a pruning saw or loppers – heavy-duty pruners.

In March, cut out all dead, diseased and weak shoots and remove suckers at the point at which they join the roots. Cut back half of the main branches to the bottom of the plant, leaving any that have strong young shoots growing near the base. Cut these main branches back to the new shoots, then shorten the young stems to about 15cm (6in).

After this initial pruning, spread a layer of well-rotted manure or compost around the plant to encourage new shoots to grow from the base; these should appear by early summer.

The following spring, repeat this procedure with the other half of the bush, then prune the rest of the plant as appropriate to the particular type of rose.

Again, after pruning, spread manure or compost around the base of the plant. The renovation process is now complete; next spring simply carry out normal pruning for the type of rose with which you are dealing.

First year

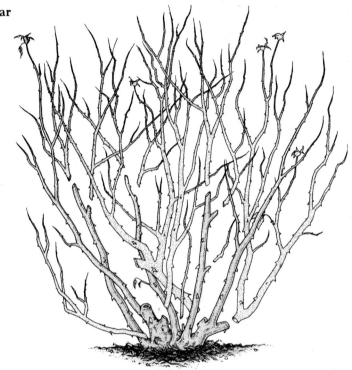

Second year

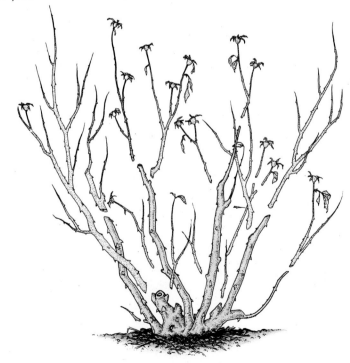

Hybrid Tea roses

Name	Height	Flower	Fragrance	Notes
Adolph Horstman	90cm (3ft)	Pink-edged yellow		Vigorous
Alec's Red	90cm (3ft)	Cherry red; full petalled	xx	Upright growth; glossy foliage
Black Beauty	120cm (4ft)	Crimson scarlet with darker undersides		Vigorous
Blessings	90cm (3ft)	Salmon pink; full; carried in clusters	x	Heavy bloomer; good for bedding
Blue Moon	90cm (3ft)	Silver lilac; large	xx	Nearest rose to blue; good for cutting
Dutch Gold	90cm (3ft)	Deep yellow gold; large	xx	Upright growth; leathery foliage
Elizabeth Harkness	75cm (30in)	Pink-edged creamy buff; large; early	x	Healthy; reliable; semi-glossy foliage
Fragrant Cloud	90cm (3ft)	Scarlet coral; dusky; colour strongest in autumn	xx	Vigorous; glossy foliage; upright growth
Just Joey	90cm (3ft)	Orange copper with red veins; ruffled petals	x	Good for bedding; vigorous, spreading growth
King's Ransom	90cm (3ft)	Rich, unfading yellow; medium size	x	Lush, glossy foliage; good for cutting
Kronenberg	120cm (4ft)	Deep crimson, yellow undersides; older flowers fade to purple	x	Very vigorous
Mme Butterfly	90cm (3ft)	Delicate blush-pink; full; carried on nearly thornless stems	xx	Good for cutting; upright growth
Mme Louise Laperrière	75cm (30in)	Deep crimson; early; non-fading	xx	Bushy growth; good for bedding
Mojave	90cm (3ft)	Rich orange, fading to pink; flowers best in autumn	xx	Upright growth; glossy, bronze-green foliage; good for cutting
Pascali	100cm (3½ft)	Pure white, moderately full; one flower per stem		best white for bedding; good for cutting
Peace	120cm (4ft)	Light yellow, flushed pink; very large		Vigorous, reliable; glossy, deep-green foliage
Piccadilly	90cm (3ft)	Yellow and scarlet; medium size; fades in hot weather		Upright growth; glossy coppery foliage
Super Star	90cm (3ft)	Brilliant vermilion, edges fading to purple		Strong, well branched growth; good for cutting

Rosa Peace

Rosa Blue Moon

Rosa Super Star

Floribunda roses

Height	Flower	Fragrance	Comments	
Anne Harkness	120cm (4ft)	Orange-saffron; double		Good for hedging; late flowering
Arthur Bell	90cm (3ft)	Yellow, fading to cream	xx	Upright growth
Chanelle	90cm (3ft)	Amber pink fading to pale pink; tea rose buds		Vigorous
English Miss	75cm (30in)	Pale pink; camellia shaped	x	Bushy; free flowering
Evelyn Fison	75cm (30in)	Brilliant scarlet		Disease resistant; dark-green foliage
Glenfiddich	75cm (30in)	Amber gold; double		Attractive, dark-green foliage; upright growth
Iceberg	150cm (5ft)	White, tinged with pink; double	x	Bushy; free flowering
Kim	45cm (18in)	Bright yellow; double		Good for front of border
Lilli Marlene	75cm (30in)	Scarlet crimson; double		Vigorous, well branched; weather resistant
Mountbatten	120cm (4ft)	Soft yellow; old-fashioned	x	Vigorous
Lavender Pinocchio	75cm (30in)	Lavender-brown; large, double		Good for cutting
Orange Sensation	75cm (30in)	Brilliant orange; large, semi-double	x	Upright growth; weather resistant
Pink Parfait	100cm (3½ft)	Creamy pink; hybrid-tea shaped	xx	Prolific; good for cutting
Queen Elizabeth	2m (7ft)	Clear pink; cup-shaped, double	x	Good for back of border; attractive glossy leaves
Southampton	100cm (3½ft)	Apricot orange; semi-double, frilled	x	Upright growth; good for bedding
Victoriana	75cm (30in)	Vermilion, with silver undersides; double	x	Sturdy growth

Fl. Anne Harkness

Fl. Iceberg

Fl. Pink Parfait

Miniature Roses[*]

Name	Height	Flowers	Notes
Baby Goldstar	37m (15in)	Creamy yellow	Flower colour can vary slightly
Baby Masquerade	45cm (18in)	Yellow, changing to red; double	Strong; free flowering; suitable as a standard
Darling Flame	30cm (12in)	Rich orange, yellow undersides; double	Bushy growth; lush, dark-green foliage
Dresden Doll	37cm (15in)	Shell-pink moss roses; double	Moss-covered buds
Green Diamond	30cm (12in)	Pink buds; lime-green flowers	Unusual
Little Buckaroo	40cm (16in)	Red with white centres; small flowers	Strong growing
Pour Toi	15cm (6in)	White, tinted creamy yellow; semi-double	Bushy growth
Sheri Anne	30cm (12in)	Orange-red	Attractive buds
Snow Carpet	20cm (8in)	White; double	Spreading; useful for ground cover
Stars and Stripes	30cm (12in)	Red and white striped; single	Very unusual
Yellow Doll	30cm (12in)	Soft yellow; double, narrow petals	Bushy growth; flowers fade to creamy white

[*]Although some miniature roses have slight fragrance, they generally lack the strong scent of many hybrid teas and floribundas

Baby Masquerade

Dresden Doll

Yellow Doll

Heathers and conifers

If you are looking for year-round interest and colour, with a minimum of maintenance, consider evergreen conifers and heathers. They fit in well with the general guideline of planting at least half of the garden with evergreens if winter bareness is to be avoided. These useful, good-natured plants need a reasonably sunny, fairly open site. To ensure free-flowering, reasonably compact heathers, a south- or west-facing border is preferable, sheltered from northerly and easterly winds to minimise frost and wind scorch. Acid soil is desirable for heathers, and essential for *Calluna vulgaris*, or ling.

For maximum effect, plant heathers in groups of several plants of one variety, either in large island beds or in drifts in borders. Flower colour from heathers is possible practically throughout the year, but consider the foliage as well as the flowers. Those with copper and gold foliage look well with red and purple flowers, and complement the greens, greys and blues or conifers. Do take advantage of the different shapes and forms that conifers offer. A tall conifer, for instance, provides a focal point in a carpet of heathers.

Heathers

Winter and spring-flowering heathers

Erica carnea Winter-flowering heather. Ht 15-30cm (6-12in); sp 30cm (12in). Lime tolerant; best in sun but can stand partial shade.
'Aurea' – deep-pink flowers; gold foliage
'Foxhollow' – pale-pink flowers; gold foliage
'King George' – carmine-pink flowers; mid-green foliage
praecox 'Rubra' – deep-red flowers; mid-dark green foliage
'Springwood White' – white flowers; bright-green foliage
'Vivellii' – deepest-red flowers; dark bronze-green foliage

Erica × darleyensis Ht and sp to 60cm (2ft). Lime tolerant; best in full sun.
'A.T. Johnson' – magenta flowers; light-green foliage
'J.H. Brummage' – mid-pink flowers; gold foliage

Erica mediterranea Mediterranean heath. Ht and sp to 60cm (2ft). Lime tolerant; needs shelter and sun.
'Brightness' – rose-pink flowers; dark-green foliage
'W.T. Rackliff' – white flowers' mid-green foliage

Erica arborea alpina Tree heath. Ht 1.5m (5ft); sp 90cm (3ft). White flowers; green foliage

Summer-flowering heathers

Daboecia cantabrica Irish heath. Ht and sp 45-75cm (18-30in). Needs acid soil.
'Alba' – white flowers; mid-green foliage
'Atropurpurea' – deep-wine flowers; bronzy green foliage

Erica cinerea Bell heather. Ht 30cm (12in); sp 40cm (16in). Needs acid soil.
'C.D. Eason' – bright-pink flowers; mid-green foliage
'Windlebrooke' – purple flowers; gold foliage turning copper

Erica ciliaris Dorset Heath. Ht and sp 50-60cm (20-24in). Neesds acid soil.
'Stoborough' – white flowers, bright-green foliage

Erica vagans. Cornish heath. Ht and sp variable. Lime tolerant.
'Lyonesse' – ht and sp 45cm (18in); white flowers; bright-green foliage
'Mrs D.F. Maxwell' – ht and sp 45cm (18in); salmon-pink flowers; mid-green foliage
'Valerie Proudley' – ht and sp 25cm (10in); white flowers; gold foliage

Autumn-flowering heathers

Calluna vulgaris Scottish heather or Ling. Ht and sp variable. Best in full sun; needs acid soil.
'Blazeaway' – ht and sp 45cm (18in); mauve flowers; gold foliage, red in winter
'County Wicklow' – ht 25cm (10in) sp 30cm (12in); double pink flowers; mid-green foliage
'Golden Feather' – ht and sp 30cm (12in); mauve flowers; gold foliage, red in winter
'H.E. Beale' – ht and sp to 60cm (2ft); double pink flowers; mid-green foliage
'Robert Chapman' – ht and sp 45cm (18in); purple flowers; gold foliage, red in winter
'Serlei Aurea' – ht and sp 60cm (2ft); white flowers; gold foliage
'Silver Queen' – ht and sp 45cm (18in); mauve flowers, woolly silver foliage
'Sir John Carrington' – ht and sp 45cm (18in); crimson flowers; gold foliage, red in winter

Planting shrubs and trees

Container-grown shrubs and trees can be set out any time soil and weather conditions are favourable, but September, October and April are the best times for evergreens. Bare-rooted shrubs, including roses, and trees are best set out in autumn or early winter, so they become acclimatised and are better able to withstand drying spring winds.

If shrubs or trees are delivered in frosty weather, store them in a cool but frost-free shed – untying any wrappings to let them breathe, but keeping the roots well covered. If the weather is mild and bare-rooted plants arrive before the ground is ready, heel them in. Soak the roots before setting them close together in a trench, firming soil well in and around their roots.

Planting procedure Prepare the ground for planting (see Chapter 5). Soak bare-rooted plants overnight before planting. Water those in containers thoroughly, allowing them time to drain, then tear away the disposable container. Very gently tease out the roots, while keeping the root ball intact – this is especially important with evergreens. Cut back to sound wood any damaged root of bare-rooted and container-grown plants.

Make a hole large enough to take the root ball, or the spread-out roots of bare-rooted plants. Plant at the same depth as before the move. Work moist potting compost, or good topsoil mixed with peat, in and around the roots or root ball. Jogging the plant gently helps to settle the soil in between the roots. Firm as filling proceeds. While you are working, keep all exposed roots covered with moist sacking or newspapers. When tying trees and shrubs for their support, always use spacers.

Pit planting To set a new shrub among those established in a border; to plant a

Dwarf and slow growing conifers

Name	Ht × sp	Position	Notes
Chamaecyparis Cypress			
lawsoniana 'Ellwoodii'	2×1m (7×3½ft)	○ ◑	Compact pyramid; grey-green or blue feathery foliage
'Ellwoods Gold'	120×60cm (4×2ft)	○	As above, but slower growing with gold-tipped branches
'Minima Aurea'	60×60cm (2×2ft)	○	Rounded pyramid; gold foliage
'Minima Glauca'	50×50cm (20×20in)	○ ◑	Rounded; dense, sea-green foliage
pisifera 'Boulevard'	120×90cm (4×3ft)	○ ◑	Broadly pyramidal; silvery blue foliage
Juniperus Juniper			
communis 'Compressa'	45×15cm (18×6in)	○ ◑	Compact column; greenish-grey foliage
'Depressa Aurea'	40×120cm (16in×4ft)	○	Prostrate; yellow foliage turning bronze-gold
horizontalis 'Blue Chip'	25×150cm (10×60in)	○ ◑	Prostrate; blue-grey feathery foliage
'Glauca'	15×120cm (6in×4ft)	○	Prostrate carpet-forming; blue-green whip-cord foliage
× *media* 'Blaauw's Variety'	120×90cm (4×3ft)	○ ◑	Vase-shaped; arching, blue-grey foliage
'Mint Julep'	90×150cm (3×5ft)	○ ◑	Semi-prostrate, arching; mint-green foliage
'Old Gold'	1.2×1.5m (4×5ft)	○	Semi-prostrate; gold foliage
squamata 'Blue Star'	40×50cm (16×20in)	○	Compact; bright steel-blue foliage
Picea Spruce			
glauca Albertiana 'Conica'	90×30cm (3×1ft)	○	Conical; grass-green foliage
pungens 'Globosa'	60×60cm (2×2ft)	○	Bushy; intense silver-blue foliage
Pinus Pine			
mugo 'Pumilo'	90×90cm (3×3ft)	○ ◑	Dwarf, semi-prostrate or bushy; light-green foliage, turning dark-green
Taxus Yew			
baccata 'Standishii'	90×20cm (3ft×8in)	○ ◑	Slow growing, column; gold-yellow foliage
Thuja *occidentalis* 'Rheingold'	120×90cm	○ ◑	Broad pyramid; feathery gold foliage, turning coppery in winter
orientalis 'Aurea Nana'	60×30cm (2×1ft)	○	Rounded; gold foliage
Tsuga Hemlock			
canadensis 'Jeddeloh'	30×60cm (1×2ft)	○ ◑	Semi-prostrate; light-green foliage

specimen shrub or tree in the lawn; and on shallow soils.

Take out a hole at least 30cm (12in) wider and 20cm (8in) deeper than the root ball. Fork plenty of rotted compost, manure or peat into the bottom of the hole, plus a handful of bonemeal. Loosen the sides of the hole with the tines of the fork at the same time; plant as previously described. On lawns, leave a collar of bare soil, to enable mulching and watering to be carried out, and to cut down on the likely competition from the grass for available food and moisture.

Immediate aftercare Keep the roots moist in prolonged dry spells, apply 9 litres (2 gallons) of water per shrub or tree at least twice a week. Syringe the foliage with clean water in the evenings during warm or windy weather. Evergreens need a bit more care; consider using proprietary anti-wilt sprays when planting. Mulch generously around all newly planted specimens in spring. Firm the soil back around any plants lifted by frost or wind.

Pruning

Ornamental trees and shrubs are pruned to keep plants healthy and promote vigour; to shape them and keep them tidy; and finally to encourage maximum flower, fruit and foliage.

General guidelines
★ Cut out any dead and diseased wood as soon as noticed, no matter what time of year.
★ Always cut back to a good bud.
Evergreens and conifers require less pruning than deciduous shrubs and trees.
★ Hard pruning usually results in strong growth, and light pruning produces less vigour but more flowers.
★ Cut out weak, spindly, straggly and overcrowded shoots. Shorten crossing stems and branches. Thin fairly drastic-

ally inward-growing shoots of dense shrubs to let in light and air.
★ Remove suckers from around the base of grafted trees and shrubs.
★ Cut reverted green shoots on variegated plants back to variegated branches, or the green shoots will take over.
★ Work to a renewal programme for deciduous flowering shrubs, cutting out a few of the oldest branches every year.

Pruning practice Flowering habit influences the way flowering shrubs are pruned. If you are unsure about flowering habit, leave the shrub in question unpruned, or pruned very lightly, for a year or two, until you can weigh up its habit.
★ *Prune after flowering* shrubs which flower on wood formed the previous one or two years. Forsythia, weigela, philadelphus and hydrangea are examples. Cut out old, worn-out flowered stems, and thin out weak or overcrowded shoots at the same time.
★ *Prune hard each spring* summer-flowering shrubs like buddleia, caryopteris and hardy fuchsia, which bloom at the tips of new wood. Cut buddleia back to older wood; cut caryopteris and some fuchsias back to soil level. Shrubs like dogwood and willow, grown for coloured bark, are also pruned hard back in spring. Some people prefer to prune biennially, but annual pruning for best colouring.

Ornamental flowering trees whether evergreen or deciduous, are pruned lightly. Once the basic framework is formed, simply thin out the branches, removing dead wood and shortening crossing stems.

Propagation

The cheapest way to fill a new garden or border quickly is by propagating your own plants. There are several methods of plant propagation, some easier than others, but all within the scope of the amateur gardener.

Division This is the easiest method of increasing herbaceous perennials, and many houseplants. It is also the least risky, provided a few basic rules are followed.

Only use healthy plants for propagation. Herbaceous plants flowering in spring are best dealt with in autumn; those flowering in summer and autumn are best dealt with from October through to March. Choose a time when the plant is resting and soil and weather conditions are favourable.

Systematically work round the clump with a fork, easing up and lifting as you go. Tease the soil, small stones and weeds from the roots. It is usually necessary to chop cleanly through large, old clumps into several pieces, using a spade. Young plants can often be pulled apart by hand. Trim up each segment with a sharp knife, cutting back any damaged roots, and discarding the worn-out centre portions. Use only weed-free, young, actively growing portions of the clump for re-planting. (The youngest growth is usually found on the outside of the clump, the older growth in the centre.) Make sure each segment has healthy, strong buds and vigorous roots.

Dust all cut surfaces thoroughly with a fungicide and re-plant promptly. Don't allow the roots to dry out; cover with wet sacking if there is the slightest delay. Always re-plant in a fresh part of the border, to avoid possible build-up of specific pests and diseases.

Lastly, dividing plants rejuvenates them as well as being a method of propagation. If herbaceous plants are to remain healthy and vigorous, they need to be lifted and divided every four or five years.

Sowing seed indoors

Although you can buy bedding plants 'ready-grown', it is less expensive, and you have a far greater range of choice, if you grow your own from seed. (Inci

SOWING SEED INDOORS

1. *Whatever container you use, place drainage material at the bottom.*

2. *Cover drainage materials with compost, firming gently.*

3. *Level the surface of the compost by pressing with a flat piece of wood.*

4. *Scatter a little seed into the tray by tapping it gently from your hand.*

5. *With large seeds, sow two in a small pot and remove the weaker seedling.*

6. *Sieve compost evenly over the newly sown seeds in the tray.*

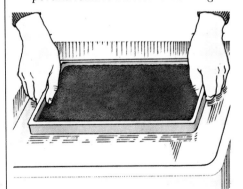

7. *Stand the tray in water until the surface looks moist.*

8. *Lift seedlings, with a dibber, to a new tray giving them room to grow on.*

dentally, use the materials and methods set out below to grow vegetables and perennial plants from seed.)

★ *Materials* Whether you use pots, half pots, seed trays or margarine cartons, there are three basic rules. The container should have a minimum depth of 5cm (2in), so it doesn't dry out; there should be drainage holes in the base; and it should be washed and sterilised before use.

Use proprietary seed compost, soil or peat-based, for the vast majority of seeds. Primulas prefer a mix of two-thirds peat and one-third sand. Always use fresh, clean compost.

★ *The method* Line the bottom of the container with a layer of clean gravel. Top to overflowing with damp seed compost. Level off with a straight-edged piece of wood. Using your fingers, firm soil-based composts round the edges and into the corners; finally firming down with the bottom of a clean jam jar to leave the surface about 1cm (½in) below the rim. Don't compress peat-based mixtures.

The methods of sowing vary to suit the seed. The vast majority of bedding plant (and vegetable) seeds are medium sized, flat or round. Taking a pinch of seed at a time, between finger and thumb, sow sparingly over the compost. Cover the seed to a depth equal to twice their diameter, by sifting over more seed compost; you will find that a sugar sifter works well.

With tiny, dust-like seeds, first cover the compost with a layer of sand, just sufficient to enable you to see the seeds. Sow very thinly; it helps to use 'V'-shaped stiff paper. Petunia, antirrhinum, lobelia and begonia seeds are sown in this way. These seeds are not covered with compost.

Pelleted and larger seeds are individually sown about 5cm (2in) apart in seed trays or singly in pots. Cover pelleted seeds with compost to a depth equal to their diameter. Large seeds like those of sweet pea and lupin are sown at a depth of two to three times their

diameter. Broad, flat seeds are sown edgeways, at a similar depth; cucumber, marrow and melon seeds are typical examples.

A few annuals – clarkia, candytuft and godetia in particular – resent root disturbance. Because of this, sow these only two or three to a small pot and subsequently thin to one.

★ *Aftercare* Water sown containers from below, to avoid disturbing the seed. Stand the containers to half their depth in a bowl of clean water, coloured the palest pink with potassium permanganate crystals. Remove as soon as the surface is visibly moist; it usually takes about 20 minutes. Drain well and then enclose the container in a clear, perforated plastic bag. Germinate on a warm windowsill or in a propagator out of direct sun.

Some seeds need to get away to an early start, and consequently need extra warmth. In the absence of a propagator it is well worth buying a soil warmer, which simply fits into the bottom of a standard seed tray.

Examine the germinating seeds regularly. Open up the plastic bag for a few hours each day as soon as there are signs of growth. Gradually increase the length of time the bag is opened, until it can be removed entirely. Shade the tender seedlings from sun, and any necessary watering should be done from below.

As soon as the seedlings are large enough to handle they are ready for pricking out. Before disturbing the seedlings, water from the bottom, and allow to drain for twenty minutes. Then, carefully handling the small plants by the leaves, gently ease them out with a lollipop stick. Either plant them singly into small pots, or 5cm (2in) apart in seed trays, using standard potting compost.

Three weeks to a month after pricking out, start feeding with half-strength, dilute liquid fertiliser. Harden off all indoor raised plants thoroughly before setting outdoors.

Taking cuttings

Plants are not difficult to raise from stem cuttings; the way cuttings are taken, and subsequently treated, vary to suit the particular plant and time of year.

★ *Guidelines* Only take cuttings from vigorous, healthy plants. Virus diseases, for instance, are transmitted in cuttings from one generation to the next. Cuttings taken from weak plants are usually reluctant to root and using them for propagation is a waste of time. Select cuttings from unflowered shoots if possible; they are easier to root. Take cuttings at the time when they are most highly charged with water – this is normally in the morning.

Remove cuttings with sharp secateurs or a sharp knife. Place them immediately into a plastic bag, to prevent wilting. (More cuttings are lost through wilting than any other single cause.) Geraniums and some cacti and succulents are the exception to the rule. These plants are far more vulnerable to rotting than they are to wilting, and they need to be dried off for about a day or two at this stage.

Fill small pots with moist cutting compost before the cuttings are taken, so the potting-up process can be as speedy as possible. Either use proprietary cutting compost, or a mixture of

SOFTWOOD CUTTINGS

1. *Cut shoot from plant with sharp blade.*

2. *Trim to just below base of leaf joint.*

3. *Remove lower leaves close to stems.*

4. *Dip into hormone rooting powder.*

5. *Carefully insert cutting into compost.*

6. *Firm around cutting with your fingers.*

7. *Water well in with fine spray.*

8. *Place in propagator or mist unit.*

9. *Alternatively, place in plastic bag.*

half and half peat and sand. As a safe-guard, dip prepared cuttings into a pro-prietary rooting preparation/fungicide before insertion into cutting compost.

Plant the cuttings up to a third of their length, in dibber holes (made with a pencil), around the edge of the pots. Four cuttings per pot is the maximum. Provide daylight, but the cuttings must be shaded from sun.

★ *Softwood cuttings* are taken from the young tip growth of plants with succu-lent stems: herbaceous perennials and houseplants. Spring is the best time, but softwood cuttings can be taken through summer. Avoid any shoots which are thick and sappy, and those which are weak and spindly. Use a razor blade to cut the base cleanly and squarely just below a leaf joint, leaving a prepared cutting of 3-8cm (1-3in) in length. Remove the lower pair of leaves; never bury leaves in the cutting compost, or rotting is inevitable. En-case the potted cuttings in an inflated clear plastic bag, securing the top with an elastic band. This creates a moist atmosphere, offsetting the loss of water through the leaves, which at this stage is always more than the base can take up. Open the bag up daily to air – and spray the cuttings regularly with tepid water.

Softwood cuttings root readily on a warm windowsill, shaded from strong sun. The bottom heat provided by a seed tray soil warmer or propagator does speed things up. Expect softwood cut-tings to root in about a month. Harden them off gradually, pot up into standard potting compost and grow on as young plants.

★ *Semi-ripe cuttings* are taken from a whole range of shrubs when the young growths have partially ripened. Take them as soon as they are ready, but old hands say as near to mid-summer as possible.

Make them a bit longer than soft-wood cuttings, up to 15cm (6in) in length. Trim the base as described for softwood cuttings, then cut out the soft tip to just above a pair of leaves. Remove the leaves from the lower half of the cutting. Many evergreen cuttings are better taken with a 'heel': a piece of old wood attached to the base. Simply pull evergreen side shoots gently away from the parent plant, and trim any ragged edges from the heel before inserting in compost.

Semi-ripe cuttings will root under cooler conditions than softwoods, and are not so prone to rotting. However, they normally root most successfully if treated in much the same way as soft-wood cuttings.

★ *Hardwood cuttings* Many ornamental shrubs, as well as gooseberries, black, red and white currants and vines, are raised from hardwood cuttings. October is a good month to take most hardwood cuttings, which are rooted in a shel-tered bed outdoors, and need to be planted while there is still some warmth in the soil.

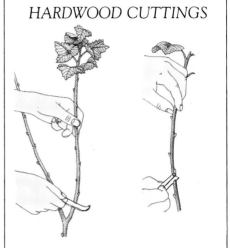

HARDWOOD CUTTINGS

Cut ripe or woody shoot and trim to 4 or 5 shoots before placing in soil.

Select sturdy healthy ripened shoots which have just completed their first year's growth. Cut cleanly near the join with the main stem, then trim the base just below a leaf joint. Alternatively, pull the cutting away with a 'heel', then neaten off any long tails of old wood.

Cut back the soft tips to a good bud, aiming for a finally prepared cutting 20-30cm (8-12in) in length. Remove any remaining leaves from deciduous cut-tings. Remove all the leaves from the lower half of evergreen cuttings. When dealing with large-leaved evergreens, cut the leaves in half crossways. Laurel and Mexican orange are two popular shrubs responding to this treatment.

Dip the cut base of each prepared cutting into proprietary hardwood rooting preparation before inserting in sand-lined dibber holes in a sheltered corner outdoors. Set the cuttings about 15cm (6in) deep and 10cm (4in) apart, firming the soil well around each cut-ting. Finally, spray evergreens with an anti-wilt preparation.

Don't allow the cuttings to dry out. Hoe from time to time, and check if they have been lifted by frost or wind, firming in as necessary. The base of the cutting must be in continual direct contact with the soil. Most cuttings are rooted and ready to move in about a year, but others take a great deal longer.

SEMI-RIPE CUTTINGS

1. *Remove lower stems from the cutting.*

2. *Gently rub off any lower leaves.*

3. *Insert the cuttings into the compost.*

Chapter 7

THE LAWN

We are fortunate in having a climate which favours the growth of grass, but lawns do not make themselves. In this chapter we look at the tried and true techniques and discuss them in detail. Is seeding the answer? Or is turfing the better bet? The pros and cons are reviewed, so that you have a sound basis to determine what is the best way to set about the job for your garden.

Unfortunately, unless given a modicum of care, lawns quickly deteriorate into a mass of weeds, moss and bare patches. If you follow the guidelines set out here you don't have to become a slave to your garden to achieve acceptable results. The main lawn care operations are described in detail: mowing, feeding, patching, spiking, moss, worm and weed control, and watering. A simple calendar of 'when to' jogs the memory.

Finally, bear in mind that a mower is likely to be the most costly item of garden equipment you will ever own – pay attention to the tips in this chapter and save yourself unnecessary disappointment and expense.

A well kept lawn is an asset to any garden. It acts as the perfect foil for beds and borders. A lawn provides a practical, economical ground cover. It is cheaper to lay than paving, although a lawn can't replace paving in every instance. Hard surfacing is always needed for areas which receive very heavy use. Grass, for instance, is unsuitable for patios and most paths. Any reasonable lawn requires a certain amount of ongoing care and attention, a point which should be taken into consideration. A lawn cannot be ignored like paving.

Laying turf

Turfing is the quickest way to make a lawn, but it is also the most expensive, and it is heavy work. Choose good-quality utility turf.

Spring and autumn are the best times to lay turf. If there is any urgency, it can be laid at other times, provided frosty, waterlogged or drought conditions are avoided.

Unless turves are to be laid within 24 hours of delivery, they should be spread out on arrival, grass-side up.

Prepare the lawn area as outlined in *July* (see page 104). Mark out the proposed lawn; use pegs and taut string for straight edges, and a trickle of sand for curves. When planning, bear in mind that gentle curves are easier to mow than sharp bends.

Start laying turves at one corner, and lay the first row in a straight line lengthways. Subsequently, stagger each row, rather like laying bricks, so that joins do not align.

Don't attempt to bend the turves into curves; lay them straight and cut off any surplus later. make sure each turf is pushed firmly against its neighbour. Constantly check levels with a straight-edge and spirit level, adding or removing soil as necessary, to correct depressions or high spots. Gently tamp each row of turves after laying with the back of a spade.

On slopes, lay turves lengthways and secure by driving in 1cm (½in) diameter, 15cm (6in) long pegs. As soon as the turves are established. Knock the pegs so that they are below the level of mower blades.

Trickle sandy potting compost between the turves, filling all spaces neatly up to surface level. This prevents undue drying out and shrinking back at the edges, and speeds up establishment. Finish by brushing the compost well in with a birch besom or stiff broom, this will cause flattened grass blades to be loosened up at the same time, which is good for them – and more attractive.

Cut edges with a half-moon edging iron or spade, at right angles to the surface. Use a plank as a guide for straight edges to leave a shoulder of 4cm (1½in).

Water immediately after turfing, and keep moist until established. Keep the joints topped up with sandy potting compost until the turves completely knit together.

When turfing a lawn, always work from a plank of wood. Never stand on newly laid turf or on the prepared soil; this is vital on heavy ground.

TYPES OF GRASS

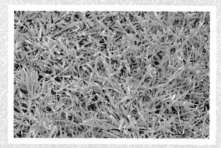

1. *Densely-tufted Chewing fescue prefers light, well-drained conditions.*

2. *Loosely-tufted wood meadow-grass grows in woods and moist places.*

3. *Hard-wearing crested dog's tail grows well on heavier chalky soil.*

4. *Browntop bent is commonly used for fine lawns and bowling greens.*

5. *Perennial rye grass is found in old pastures and valued as a hay-maker.*

6. *Timothy grass is shallow-rooting and, like rye, valued as a hay-maker.*

LAYING A TURF LAWN

1. Keeping the edges straight, begin to lay the turf along one side of the lawn.

2. Turf should be cut with a sharp half-moon edging iron or a sharp knife.

3. When filling in the turves, lay them as close together as possible.

4. Ensure turves are level with the ground (or follow the slope).

5. Place more soil under low turves or remove soil from high ones.

6. Tamp down the newly-laid turves to firm them in to place.

7. A newly-turfed lawn has a brickwork pattern which later knits together.

8. With a stiff broom lift the flattened grass and brush in the top dressing.

9. Creating a lawn is hard work, but the finished product is well worth it.

Seeding a lawn

As with turf, a good quality utility mixture is a sound choice. Problem gardens may need a shade-tolerant mixture or one which is extra hard-wearing. Buy sufficient grass seed to sow at the rate of 50g per sq m (1 ½oz per sq yd).

April sowing is usually successful, but watering needs watching after spring sowings. Late August/September is the best time, when there is still some warmth remaining in the soil, thus enabling the young seedlings to get off to a good start in life.

Prepare the ground as outlined in *July* (see page 104). Choosing a calm, mild day, mark out the lawn into m (yd) wide strips, using pegs and string. To avoid damaging the seed bed, especially on heavy soils, work from planks; a modern, lightweight plank can be useful. Lightly rake before sowing. The soil should be moist, but just beginning to dry on the surface.

Divide the seed allocation for each strip into two. Sow half, as evenly as possible, up and down, and the remainder across the strip; this ensures a more even distribution. Sow each strip in a similar manner, seeding to about 8cm (3in) beyond the intended lawn

area, to allow for trimming and shaping. Remove the strings and lightly rake in the seeds, no deeper than 3mm (⅛in). Keep the handle of the rake nearly vertical or the seed is easily buried too deeply. On heavy soil, cover the seed with potting compost rather than raking in. Finally, very gently tamp down the soil with the back of the rake, holding the handle upright. Protect the seed bed from birds, even if you have used seed impregnated with bird repellent; criss-cross dark coloured thread, attached to pegs, 8cm (3in) above the entire surface. Lightly water the whole lawn and be sure to keep it moist until shoots begin to appear.

SEEDING A LAWN

1. Remove all debris from site, then dig and manure.

2. Break down the surface with a fork.

3. Tread evenly over the soil to firm, then rake.

4. Sow the grass seed evenly, releasing it very slowly.

5. Divide the ground, and seed, into equal parts for accurate sowing.

6. Rake seed in – across the previous furrows.

Month-by-month lawn care

January

Keep off the lawn when wet or frozen. Rake up any leaves or debris when conditions are favourable. Spike any wet muddy patches.

Put your mower in for overhaul.

Buying a new mower

★ *Which mower?* Cylinder mowers give the best cut, for high-quality turf and for hardwearing lawns. Dry, coarse grass stalks will be left uncut, though, and the odd cut or two with a rotary mower, or clipping with shears, is needed during the growing season for all but the finest lawns.

Rotary mowers are ideal for rough grass, banks and verges, and they do a reasonable job on hardwearing lawns. They are not intended for high-class lawns. Choose a model with a rear roller if you want the much sought after dark and light striped effect. After being cut for some time with non-roller mowers, lawns do become 'puffy', and benefit

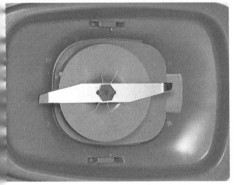

A rotary *mower*

A cylinder *mower*

from rolling once or twice during the growing season. The smaller rotaries don't have grass-collecting facilities, and although most present-day models chop up the grass very finely, clippings are still best gathered. If left on the lawn, clippings encourage weeds, disease and worms.

Cord cutters are the answer to those awkward areas near the base of walls and trees.

Very few hand-pushed, or manual, mowers are sold these days. Electric mowers are the most popular, and they are more than justified on any area over 40sq m (48sq yd). About 60m (200ft) of flex is the absolute maximum; for areas further away from the power source than this, petrol-driven models need to be considered. They work out more costly, but may be the best option.

February

If the weather is favourable, begin soil preparations for seeding at the end of the month.

Given a mild season, worm activity can become evident in warmer districts; scatter worm casts with a stiff brush or besom.

Spike any wet areas and top-dress with sand.

Spiking

Spiking is simply a means of perforating the topsoil, and relieving compaction. It is needed on most lawns, but especially on those areas which get extra-heavy use. Spiking improves drainage and allows more air and moisture to reach grass roots. If sand or potting compost is brushed into the spike holes, soil texture is also improved.

Spiking can be carried out on compacted lawns at almost any time, but as a mater of routine, try to spike annually each autumn.

A garden fork is the tool normally used. Push it down vertically, to a depth of 10cm (4in) and gently rock it to and

Aeration of lawns can be done quickly and easily using mechanical spikes.

fro before removing. Systematically work across the problem area, spiking at 15cm (6in) intervals. A hollow-tine fork is useful for badly compacted or very heavy soil. Plugs of soil are removed by the tines, and need to be raked up. Reserve powered mechanical spikers for large lawns; consider hiring one for the day. Hand-pushed models are heavy work.

March

Choosing a time when both weather and soil conditions are favourable, gently rake off all surface debris and stones.

Lawns may suffer from frost heave during winter, and benefit from a light rolling to settle them back at this time of year.

When grass growth is obvious, give the first cut of the season, with the blades set high. Mow only in dry weather, and never overdo mowing in March; one or two cuts should be ample.

If moss is getting troublesome, apply moss-killer. If there are an intolerable number of worms, apply worm-killer; if the problem is small scale, simply scatter the casts. Treat the diseases snow mould and red thread at the first

signs of attack: patches of dead or dying grass, with a growth of cottony white mould are typical of snow mould; patches of weak-growing grass with red cotton-like threads signal red thread. Both respond to being drenched with fungicide.

Start spring feeding, at the end of the month in mild areas.

Neaten lawn edges by cutting down vertically with a half-moon edging iron or spade; use a plank as a straightedge. A weekly clipping with shears should then suffice throughout the remainder of the season.

In mild areas complete pre-sowing/turfing preparations, by applying a pre-seeding fertiliser. Don't attempt to sow or turf a lawn before the end of this unpredictable month.

Repairing boken edges

Although this can be done at any time, apart from the height of summer and the depths of winter, now is one of the best times to tackle the job. Cut out a square of the damaged turf, under-cutting with a spade, and aiming for an even thickness throughout. Move the turf forward and straighten off by cutting against a straight-edged plank in line with the rest of the lawn edge. Fill the space behind the turf with potting compost, firm and sow. Protect from birds, which have a habit of using these areas as bird-baths.

Repairing damaged areas

Bare patches can be re-seeded quite simply by scarifying heavily and vigorously, with a wire rake, then top-dressing with potting compost and sowing. If disease is suspected of being the main cause of trouble, cut out the turf, to a depth of 4cm (1½in). Infill with potting compost, firm and sow. Lightly rake in and water, and protect from birds. If turves are available, these make an instant repair. Always match up the seed mixture or turf as nearly as possible to the existing lawn. Any mixture of textures may look unsightly.

New lawn edges

A proprietary lawn edging strip tapped into place around a newly trimmed lawn (see pages 98-99) effectively prevents damage. These edgings are available in plastic or metal, and are quite attractive. The top of the strip should be slightly lower than the lawn, for ease of mowing.

Lawns taken right up to a wall are difficult to mow and lead to grazed knuckles. Remove a narrow strip of turf between the lawn and wall; this strip can be paved or made into a flower bed.

Try to maintain a small dip where lawn meets flower-bed, so that edges can be neatly maintained.

Maintain a collar of bare earth around the base of trees and shrubs growing in lawns, treating the edge as for the rest of the lawn. This not only looks better than faded grass, but newly planted trees and shrubs won't suffer from the competition of grass growing close into their stems.

April

Continue to turf and seed new lawns on prepared sites. Keep recently seeded or turfed areas well but gently watered.

Continue to patch and repair lawns as for March.

Start routine spring feeding.

Apply weed-killer and moss-killer if necessary.

Start routine mowing.

Mowing

Cut fine lawns twice a week, hard-wearing lawns once. When they are growing freely in spring, hardwearing lawns also benefit from two cuts.

Before mowing, remove loose stones, wire and similar debris by hand. Postpone mowing if the lawn is wet.

In spring and autumn, worms are likely to be active; spread any worm casts with a wire rake before starting to mow. Pull up grass blades with a wire rake, teasing up creeping weeds like clover at the same time. After repeated teasing and cutting, the growth of these weeds is eventually weakened.

Tie up temporarily any nearby plants in danger of being damaged by the mower.

Adjust the cutter blades. Cut hard-wearing lawns at 2.5cm (1in) at the start of the season, and during hot dry weather in mid-summer. Lower the blades to 18mm (¾in) at other times. Fine lawns are cut slightly closer.

With electric mowers, start cutting near the power point and work away from it. This reduces the chances of getting tangled up in the cable.

Vary the direction of cut each time the lawn is mown; work down, diagonally and across on subsequent occasions.

Even in the best managed garden, long grass may occasionally need dealing with. Mow long grass in two stages: top it first with the mower set high, then reduce the height of the blades for the second cut.

Finally, trim the edges. Long-handled edging shears are useful for the purpose, and reduce the need to bend. For a general purpose tool, ordinary hand shears are better; they can be used for trimming edges, clipping hedges, and trimming long grass on banks and in awkward places. Electric edge trimmers make light work where they can be justified.

Lawn feeding

Lawn feed is applied in either liquid or granular form, or as a top dressing (discussed in September). Always select a proprietary balanced feed to suit the time of year.

On most lawns one spring or summer feed will normally suffice. For best results, apply the feed now, though it can be given, provided conditions are favourable, right up to the beginning of August. A second feed in summer should follow a spring feed only if growth is sluggish, and even then give a much lighter dressing.

When spring comes, it doesn't take much effort to get a lawn into shape.

It is usually risky to feed in autumn, but if the lawn is starved, or on light, sandy soil, go ahead, provided you use an 'autumn' compound fertiliser. Other fertilisers are liable to result in lush, disease-prone growth.

Never apply fertiliser to dry soil; water the lawn if necessary, a couple of days beforehand. Don't feed during drought, or the grass is liable to scorch.

★ *Application* To broadcast dry fertiliser by hand, first mark out the area into manageable strips of equal size with pegs and string – otherwise it is easy to overlap or miss areas. Systematically fertilise each strip, spreading half the allocated amount in one direction and half in the other. It helps to mix the feed with dry sand, or use a feed which has been coloured to make distribution easier. Alternatively, use a fertiliser distributor, working systematically to and fro across the lawn. Again, don't overlap or leave gaps. Liquid feed can be simply applied with a watering can and dribble bar. A modern hose-end dilutor fits on to a watering can and hose, and is much quicker for feeding large areas, whether lawn or flower beds.

May

Lower mower blades, and cut at least every week.

Top-dress joints in newly turved lawns (see June).

Continue to lay turf, and to feed established lawns.

This is the best month for weed-killing.

Weed-killing

Be ruthless with weeds. They not only compete with grass for valuable food, moisture and air, but make conditions favourable for pests and diseases.

Don't worry about annual weeds appearing on new lawns; they quickly succumb once mowing begins. Remove perennial, deep-rooted weeds by hand.

★ *Weed-killer application* Hormone weed-killers should be applied between spring and late summer, when the weeds are actively growing. Don't apply them during a drought, in wet spells, or to areas newly seeded within the past six months.

Start by liquid feeding a week before the intended application. Four days before, mow the lawn. Pick a calm, mild day to apply the weed-killer, when the soil is moist and the grass dry. Before you begin, tease the weed leaves into an upright position with a rake.

Dilute the liquid weed-killer and apply evenly over the lawn; a dribbling bar fitted to a watering can is an efficient way of doing this. Take care there is no drift or spillage on to garden plants. Leave for three days, then mow.

A watering can with a dribbling bar enables you to apply moss- or weed-killer evenly.

Don't put the clippings on the compost heap.

Avoid using dry hormone weed-killers which incorporate fertilisers if the soil is dry. It is safest to apply these chemicals with a fertiliser distributor to avoid overlap. Although the mixture provides labour-saving ways of weeding and feeding at the same time, better results are often possible if feeding is applied some days beforehand.

If there are only a few isolated weeds, spot treat or hand weed them. Choose from proprietary paint, dab-on gels, waxes or aerosol cans which direct the spray into the crown of each weed.

Moss-killing

Either use lawn sand or a proprietary liquid moss-killer. Lawn sand is applied between the end of April and mid-June. This is a contact weed-killer and as well as killing moss, it takes care of some broad-leaved weeds, and feeds the lawn. Don't walk on the lawn after lawn sand has been applied until it has been wet; water if no rain has fallen after two days or so. After about three weeks the dead moss should be ready for raking up. Re-seed any bare patches, and set about improving general growing conditions, to discourage the further growth of moss.

Proprietary liquid moss-killers are more versatile and can be applied in spring, autumn or late winter.

June

If growth becomes lush, mow twice a week. If there are prolonged dry spells, raise the height of the cutter bar.

Treat weeds as necessary, spot treating any left behind from earlier applications of weed-killer.

Summer feed if lawns look jaded or spring feeding was missed out.

In hot, dry weather spike and water. Start preparing ground for lawns to be laid in early autumn.

Give new lawns their first cut.

Cutting newly seeded lawns

When grass is about 4cm (1½in) high, hand pick stones, removing everything over 1cm (½in) in diameter. Lightly roll; the back roller of a cylinder mower will suffice. Wait for a couple of days, to allow the seedlings to spring back up, then top off 1cm (½in) of growth. Hand shears are best; you can use a cylinder mower with the blades set high, but some grass is bound to be uprooted. Either way, the blades must be sharp.

New lawn problems

★ *Surface cracking* in dry weather is not uncommon, especially on heavy soils which have not been watered enough. Spike with a fork, water gently but thoroughly, then top-dress with potting compost, brushing it well into the cracks. Sow again if necessary.

★ *Turves shrinking* back from the edges can become a problem, if they were not butted firmly together when being laid. Again, water, fill in the cracks with potting compost, and, in severe cases, the filled-in cracks.

★ *Uneven settlement* can be a problem on under-prepared sites. (See September.)

★ *Thin grass* is corrected by scarifying, applying a top-dressing and re-sowing.

July

Water if dry weather is prolonged and water restrictions permit.

Remember to tease up clover and other creeping weeds before mowing.

Push ahead with preparatory work for autumn seeding and turfing.

Ground preparations for sowing and turfing

Start preparing the bed at least three months beforehand.

Drain and level the area as necessary, so the final level of the lawn is 2.5cm (1in) or so above the level of surrounding paths. Both plants and lawn should be below the level of the damp-proof course of the dwelling. In your calculations allow for turves to be 3cm (1¼in) thick. Don't attempt to sow or turf slopes of more than 1 in 3 if you intend to mow them.

Dig the entire lawn area, removing stones and perennial weeds. Allow the soil to settle for a few weeks, then spread a layer of equal parts peat and sand, to a depth of about 2.5cm (1in). Double this on heavy soil.

Fork this lightly into the top few inches. Rake to a fine tilth, removing stones and smoothing out any minor hollows and humps. Firm with a light roller, or tread heel-to-toe fashion. Be sure to only work the ground during fine weather. Repeat this firming and raking process every few weeks. Finally, two weeks before sowing or turfing, apply balanced fertilizer at the rate of a handful per sq m (sq yd), raking well in.

August

Continue to water lawns in dry spells.

Sow new lawns at the end of the month.

This is the last opportunity to summer feed and apply weed-killer.

Watering

Start watering before the soil begins to crack and the grass turns yellow and wilts. Water thoroughly about once a week in dry weather, but water every three days in a prolonged hot spell. Give at least 1cm (½in) water at each application; standing a jam jar under the spray line gives a reasonably accurate guide. If watering with a can, allow 10 litres per sq m (2 gallons per sq yd). Resist the temptation to water daily, a practice which encourages moss, disease and shallow rooting. Shallow-rooted grasses suffer severely should you stop watering before the rains come.

Whatever type of watering equipment you choose, a fine spray is always better than a deluge of water.

Sprinklers: rotary (top); *oscillating* (above), *good for corners; perforated hose* (right), *good for long borders.*

Sprinklers range from simple, yet effective spikes which water a circle of approximately 3m (10ft) to popular rotaries, ideal for the average garden, to the more powerful pulsating models which cover an area of 200sq m (250sq yd). Finally, for awkward spots, consider a nozzle to fit on to the end of the hose. These are surprisingly effective when the hose is tied to a fork pushed into the ground.

September

Reduce the number of mowings and raise the cutter bar.

This is the best month to sow seeds. Begin laying turf.

Look for signs of snow mould and fusarium and apply fungicide (see March).

Apply worm-killer if necessary.

Try to find time to scarify, spike and top-dress your lawn.

Scarifying, spiking and top-dressing

Scarifying teases out dead grass and moss. If left to accumulate, these form a layer on the surface, commonly referred to as 'thatch', which suffocates grass and encourages disease and moss.

Scarifying is best carried out during mild spells in spring and autumn, but neglected lawns benefit at almost any time, except when the ground is frozen, waterlogged, or very dry. A wire-tined rake is the ideal tool. Work systematically from one end of the lawn to the other, and then back across the direction of the first sweep. A power-driven rotorake is a very effective implement.

Before top-dressing, always scarify the lawn to aerate the surface. After scarifying, spike the lawn (see February), then top-dress.

John Innes No 2 potting compost is ideal. It is better to make two light applications than one heavy application, allowing a minimum of a fortnight between. Apply 1kg (2lb) per sq m (yd), placing small heaps of compost evenly over the lawn and spreading them in with the back of a rake. Brush the compost well into the spike holes with a stiff brush or besom.

Repairs

The grass is liable to become sparse and faded under mature trees and shrubs. Move edges of the lawn back to tidy things up.

High and low spots. Lower high spots, or raise hollows, by slitting the turf in an 'H' cut and rolling back the flaps. Adjust the level by removing surplus soil or adding more. Replace the turf, lightly tamping with the back of a spade. Fill the joints with potting compost and water thoroughly.

If a hollow is slight, simply scarify and top-dress with compost. Repeated over a period of years, this should rectify the position. Don't add more than 1cm (½in) of compost at a time unless you are prepared to re-sow.

October

This is one of the best months of the year for you to lay turf.

Raise the cutter bar for the last few cuts of the season, and brush off any dew before mowing.

Rake up fallen leaves.

Top off newly seeded lawns (see June). In colder areas it is best to delay until spring.

November

Clean, oil and put away the lawnmower.

Clear the lawn of fallen leaves and debris, when the weather is favourable.

This is another good month for laying turf, in mild conditions.

Dig over new site for spring lawns.

December

Keep off the lawn when it is frozen or wet, but rake leaves in mild spells.

Apply fungicide if disease is troublesome.

Spike and sand compacted wet areas.

Chapter 8

FRUIT AND VEGETABLES

With a little ingenuity and imagination, a wide range of crops can be grown in odd corners of most gardens. What about in borders? Or on the patio? Or against walls and fences? Much of this chapter is devoted to salads and vegetables and advice is given on the choice of suitable varieties.

Vegetables are grouped according to their nature and needs. Ways and means of making the most of small spaces and keeping up a succession of crops, with notes on useful dodges like catchcropping and growbags, are most helpful to today's gardener with little space – or time.

Finally, the tree and berry fruits are considered, including individual crop-care notes and details of planting, feeding and pruning. All that awaits you are good harvests and even better eating!

Making the most of small space

The basic guidelines for maximum food production are twofold: to plant every bit of available space, and to ensure that each area is cropped to best advantage. However, cropping for most is a compromise situation – utilising space not taken up by decorative plants. Consider growing fruit on walls and fences; vines on overhead rafters of sheltered patios; container growing for hard surfaces; fruit bushes and trees on the lawn; odd pockets between flowers and shrubs; and, if you are lucky, a traditional vegetable patch.

Go for modern, high-yielding varieties of fruit and vegetables, selecting those which are compact, and take up little space. Be prepared to give extra care and attention to detail throughout cultivation; the more intensive the cropping, the more important this becomes if plants are not to succumb to pests and diseases.

Vegetables

Heavy crops from small plots Not all vegetables are equally suitable for small gardens. Parsnips, winter broccoli, Brussels sprouts and main-crop potatoes take up the ground for too long a time, preventing a quick turn round of crops. Since they can usually be obtained from shops, quite reasonably, and without undue loss of quality and flavour, they are rarely considered worthwhile. As a rule, small-space gardeners tend to concentrate on a selection of quick-growing crops which yield well when packed in closely together. Herbs such as mint, sage and thyme are usually planted permanently in an odd corner, in a bed of their own.

Salads and vegetables to grow In the table beginning below are listed some of the more popular crops for small gardens, with details of their requirements.

Crop notes For practical purposes, vegetable crops are usually grouped together according to their needs and cultural requirements.

Vegetables and salad crops

Crop	Light	Sow	Plant	Harvest	Spacing in bed	Container size	No per container
Bean – dwarf	○ ◑	4	5	7-8	20×45cm (8×18in)	25cm (10in)	6
Bean – runner	○ ◑	4	6	8-10	30×150cm (12×60in)	40cm (16in)	6-8
Beetroot – round	○ ◑	4-7	–	6-10	10×30cm (4×12in)	25cm (10in)	6
Cabbage – spring	○ ◑	7-8	9	3-5	45×45cm (9×18in)	–	–
Carrot – early	○ ◑	3-7	–	6-10	5×30cm (2×12in)	25cm (10in)	15
Celery – self-blanching	○ ◑	4	6	8-9	23×23cm (9×9in)	–	–
Cucumber – ridge	○ ◑	4	6	8-9	60×90cm (2×3ft)	25cm (10in)	1
Lettuce – various	○ ◑	3-6	5-7	6-10	25×25cm (10in×10in)	Growbag	8
Marrow/Courgette – bush	○ ◑	4	6	8-10	60×90cm (2×3ft)	25cm (10in)	1
Melon – cantaloupe	○ ◑	4	6	8-9	60×90cm (2×3ft)	25cm (10in)	1
Onion bulb sets	○	–	4	7-8	10×15cm (4×6in)	25cm (10in)	6-8
salad	○ ◑	4-8	–	6-10	1×15cm (½×6in)		
Potato – early	○ ◑	–	3-4	6-7	30×60cm (12×24in)	25cm (10in)	2

★ *Root crops* include beetroot and carrots. These are best grown on land manured for a previous crop, and are only given fertiliser before planting. Potatoes are the exception and are usually manured. In general, do not grow roots on freshly limed soil.

★ *Green crops* include spring cabbage. These crops need firm, well limed land, not too heavily manured, but with an application of fertiliser before planting. Lime is normally given once every three years to ground used for vegetables, and ideally goes on before setting out cabbages or greens. Don't lime chalk soils.

There is no substitute for fresh herbs. They can take remarkably little space and most grow well in the garden.

Crop	Light	Sow	Plant	Harvest	Spacing in bed	Container size	No per container
Radish – summer	○ ◑	3-9	–	4-10	1×25cm (½×10in)	25cm 10in	20
Spinach – perpetual	○ ◑	4-7	–	7-4	23×30cm (9×12in)	25cm (10in)	6-8
Sweet corn	○	4	5-6	8-9	30×40cm (12×16in)	–	–
Sweet pepper	○	3	5-6	8-9	30×45cm (12×18in)	20cm (8in)	1
Tomato Bush	○	4	5	7-10	45×45cm (18×18in)	20-25cm (8-10in)	1
tall	○	3	5-6	8-10	45×75cm (18×30in)	20-25in (8×10in)	1

Beetroot

Radish

Onion

Herbs

Crop	Nature	Height	Light	Sow	Plant	Spacing	Propagation
Chives	HP	15-30cm (6-12in)	○ ◑	4-6	Spring or Autumn	25×25cm) (10×10in)	Division
Garlic	HBb	30-90cm (1-3ft)	○	–	3 or 10	20×30cm (8×12in)	Bulb segments (cloves)
Mint	HP	45cm (18in)	◑	3-4	Spring or Autumn	20×30cm (8×12in)	Division
Parsley – curled	HB/HHB	15-20cm (6-8in)	○ ◑	2-4 or 7	Spring or Autumn	15×20cm (6×8in)	Seed only
Sage	HSh	60cm (2ft)	○	4-5	Spring or Autumn	50×50cm (20×20in)	Cuttings
Thyme – common	HSh	10-25cm (4-10in)	○	4-5	Spring or Autumn	30×50cm (12×20in)	Division

Garlic   Thyme   Mint

★ *Pod/seed and stem crops* include beans, onions, sweet corn and celery. These benefit from generous manuring plus pre-planting applications of fertiliser.

★ *Fruiting crops* include tomatoes and cucumbers. These need the warmest sites, and are normally either manured and given a pre-planting fertiliser application, or they are grown in containers of fresh potting compost.

Individual crops The following is a brief cultivation guide to vegetable crops most suitable for small-space gardeners.

★ *Bean – dwarf* Pod crop. Sow seeds 5cm (2in) apart in trays and germinate indoors in slight warmth. Harden off under a cold frame for a fortnight before

Bamboo canes and string provide a support system which is more than adequate for dwarf-type french beans.

SUPPORTING RUNNER BEANS

Staking runner beans by a wigwam of poles drawn together and fastened at the top.

The most common way of staking is to use poles made of larch wood or heavy-grade bamboo.

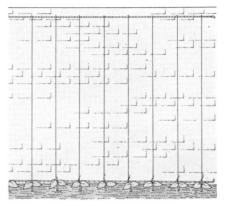

Beans can be grown up a wall by erecting a 'fence' of strings to which they can cling.

planting out in the open. Give support with twiggy pieces of stick pushed among plants. Keep continually moist. Harvest the pods while young and tender.
★ *Bean – runner* Pod crop. Sow the seeds singly in small pots and germinate indoors in warmth. Harden off as for dwarf beans before planting out in a sheltered, warm spot. Provide tall bean sticks, wires or trellis support. Mulch

Streamline runner beans produce vigorous plants over a long period.

the plants generously. Water freely in dry weather. Harvest the pods while young and tender; frequent harvesting encourages heavier cropping.
★ *Beetroot* Roop crop. Sow quick-maturing globe varieties in shallow drills outdoors, and subsequently thin. Harvest when tennis ball size or less.

Twist their leaves off (see below), don't cut them, or bleeding and loss of colour will occur.
★ *Spring cabbage* Green crop. Sow in a shallow drill in a nursery bed or in a seed tray. Transplant to cropping positions when about 10cm (4in) high, and firm in well. Thin out before leaves touch in the row, by removing alternate plants to use as greens. Use the main crop when hearted.

SOWING & HARVESTING BEETROOT

Beetroot seed capsules must be sown thinly at intervals (left above) and when harvested (left), their tops must be pulled off to prevent 'bleeding'.

HARVESTING & STORING CARROTS

New Red Intermediate (above) *is a good carrot for winter storing. When harvested, they must be eased up gently with a fork* (right top) *and stored indoors, packed head to tail between layers of dry sand.*

★ *Carrot* Root crop. Sow quick-maturing, round or stump-rooted varieties. Sow very thinly to avoid the need to thin, as thinning attracts carrot fly. If carrot fly has been troublesome, rake in a root insecticide before sowing. Harvest the roots early.

★ *Celery – self-blanching* Stem crop. Sow the seed in a pot, and germinate in warmth indoors. Prick out the seedlings, 4cm (1½in) apart, into trays. Harden off under a frame before planting outdoors in blocks, so that the leaves of the plants shade and blanch each other. The ideal place to plant is in the base of a garden frame, otherwise shade the outside rows with straw. Water freely and liquid feed generously. Harvest as soon as usable.

★ *Cucumber* Fruiting crop. Sow the seed of ridge cucumber varieties singly in small pots, and germinate at 16-18°C (60-65°F). Harden off and set out each plant on a small mound of well prepared soil or potting compost, under a cloche or frame. Underlay fruits with thin pieces of wood to keep them clean.

★ *Lettuce* Stem crop. Make successional sowings in containers, using summer varieties suitable for maturing outdoors. Prick out 4cm (1½in) apart into trays or, better still, singly into small pots. Harden off and plant outdoors or under cloches for crops early and late in the season. Start harvesting each batch before they are fully ready.

★ *Marrow* Fruiting crop. Choose quick-maturing bush varieties. Sow, harden off and plant out as for cucumbers. Pollinate the female flowers (those with tiny embryo fruits beneath the petals) by snapping off the male flowers and removing their petals. Transfer the pollen (the yellow dust) to

Little Gem or Sugar Cos (right), *is sown mid-spring to late summer for mid-summer to mid-autumn cutting; Unrivalled* (above right) *can be sown little and often for spring to autumn cutting.*

Marrows require moist, well-drained, humus-rich soil and good sunlight.

the centres of each female flower. Protect the developing fruits.

★ *Melon* Fruiting crop. Sow a cantaloupe variety, and raise the plants as for cucumbers. Plant out in a shaded frame on a raised mound of well prepared soil or potting compost. Pinch out the growing point when six leaves have formed. Allow the four best side shoots to develop and pinch out the growing points of these at the seventh leaf. Remove all the other weaker side shoots growing out from the main stem, and shorten the secondary side shoots (those growing out from the side shoots) back to one leaf. Pollinate as for marrow. Dry off the plants when the fruits are almost ripe.

★ *Onion* Stem crop. Plant sets (immature bulbs) outdoors on firm, rich ground. Bend over the tops when the leaves begin to yellow to hasten ripening, and lift as soon as the tops are almost dried. Dry off indoors and store

SOWING & HARVESTING ONIONS

Onion sets must be set into shallow drills (above far left) and, when this is completed, covered with soil simply by shuffling along the drill (above centre). The onions are ready for lifting and drying when their tops fall over (left), and they must then be eased up gently with a fork (above) and then dried, spaced apart, on wire netting, with their roots facing south.

113

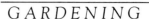
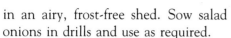

in an airy, frost-free shed. Sow salad onions in drills and use as required.

★ *Potato* Root crop. About six to eight weeks before planting, spread out the tubers of early varieties in shallow types, then stand them in a light, airy, frost-free shed to sprout. Plant 10-15cm (4-6in) deep in drills or individually, with a dibber. Earth up each time the shoots put on about 13cm (5in) of growth, until the plants meet between the rows. Start lifting as soon as the potatoes are large enough to use, usually when the flowers appear.

★ *Radish* Stem crop. Make successive sowings in shallow drills, using round or oval, quick-maturing summer varieties. Keep well watered and encourage the crop to grow quickly, or hot-flavoured, woody roots are likely. Harvest young.

★ *Spinach* Stem crop. Sow in shallow drills where the crop is to mature, and subsequently thin to final spacing. Harvest regularly, taking just a few leaves at a time.

★ *Sweet corn* Pod crop. Sow seeds singly in small pots of weak potting compost. Germinate and keep at 16-18°C (60-65°F). Harden off before planting out in a favourable spot, in blocks of twelve or more. Earth up stems for extra support. Harvest when the tassels change colour, and the kernels are firm and milky. Press your thumb nail into a kernel to test.

Sweet Corn (right) *is a subtropical plant and is grown as a half-hardy annual in temperate climates; it needs at least 3 months of warm weather to do well. Perpetual* (above right), *like all types of spinach, requires a sunny site and soil which is humus-rich and moisture-retentive and also well-drained.*

INTERCROPPING

If radishes are sown when cabbages are planted out, the radishes will be ready to be picked in about 4 weeks, leaving more room for the cabbages to develop and mature. They will be ready for picking in another 4-5 weeks.

EASY-GROWN TOMATOES

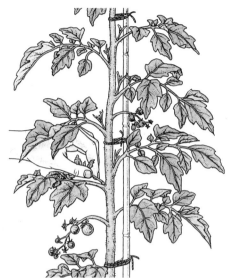

1. The branches develop extra shoots where they must be broken off (side shooting) before they are 3cm (1in) long.

2. When 4 or 5 bunches of tomato flowers (trusses) have formed, cut off the growing stem above the highest truss.

3. If there is no room in the ground to grow tomatoes, plastic, compost-filled growing bags are an excellent substitute.

★ *Sweet pepper* Fruiting crop. Sow indoors in pots and germinate at 16-18°C (60-65°F). Prick out singly into small pots and grow on in warmth. Pot on into 15-20cm (6-8in) pots for indoor growing, or harden off and plant out under a garden frame or cloche. Pinch out the growing point when about 15cm (6in) high. Stake and tie. Harvest the fruits when green, or leave until ripe.

★ *Tomato* Fruiting crop. Sow, germinate and prick out as for sweet peppers. Harden off and plant out in a favoured site outdoors; they do best under a frame or against a sunny wall. Tall varieties need staking and tying and to have their side shoots removed. Pinch out the growing points at the second leaf above the fourth flower/fruit truss. Harvest fruits as the colour changes, to hasten the ripening of the remainder of the crop. Bush varieties are neither stopped nor side shooted, but they do benefit from some support.

'Marmande' (top left) *is a very large succulent beefsteak tomato;* *'Gardener's Delight'* (left) *has been called the tastiest of all tomatoes.*

Cropping in small space

Rotating crops When planning your cropping programme try, where possible, to group like with like. Keep all the root crops together, and, similarly, the pod and stem crops. This makes it easier to manage the soil from the manuring and liming aspects, and helps with crop rotation (see page 116). Do not grow any one group of crops in the same bit of ground, more than once every three years. This minimises the risk of pests and diseases. Herbs are somewhat different; many are perennial and crop happily year after year without being disturbed. However, when planting garlic or parsley, practise rotation; give them a fresh piece of ground each year.

Fruiting crops like tomatoes, which need the same sunny, sheltered part of the garden each year, can be grown in containers, to avoid 'sickening' the soil. The other alternative is to adopt the commercial growers' practice of disinfecting the soil. This is feasible by drenching the soil with a cresylic acid

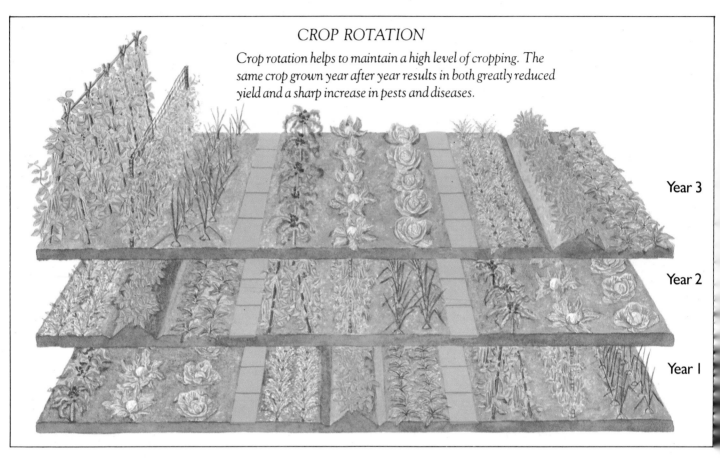

CROP ROTATION

Crop rotation helps to maintain a high level of cropping. The same crop grown year after year results in both greatly reduced yield and a sharp increase in pests and diseases.

Year 3

Year 2

Year 1

preparation like Jeyes Fluid prior to setting out the plants.

Keeping up a succession In small gardens where space is at a premium, it is doubly important that the interval between crops is minimal. Don't allow the ground to lie idle for longer than is absolutely essential. Don't wait for one crop to finish before deciding on the next. Plan well in advance. Wherever possible, have partially-grown plants in containers, ready and waiting to take the place of growing crops as they finish. For example, self-blanching celery or sweet corn, sown in April and grown on in pots or trays, should be ready to plant out in June, to follow a harvested crop of early lettuce or spring cabbage.

Catchcropping Planting a quick-growing catch crop of lettuce or radish, between lifting early potatoes in June or July and planting spring cabbage in September, makes full use of the land.

Intercropping This is one of the most valuable techniques available to the gardener with limited space. Intercropping involves growing two crops, usually at different stages of maturity, side by side. The main crop may be runner beans or tomatoes. These are interplanted with lettuce or radish. The lettuce and radish are ready to harvest well before the main crop, and don't interfere with it.

Intercropping can be modified to work well among perennial plants and shrubs, provided there is adequate space and light for the intercrop to grow. Make sure the ground is well cultivated and extra fertiliser added to sustain the crop.

Many of the crops mentioned in the table can be grown successfully as intercrops. Runner beans can be grown at the back of a border. Try growing beetroot or carrots as an edging or among ornamental plants; they both have attractive foliage. Lettuce and radish, interplanted in a perennial

border in early spring, should be cleared by the time the herbaceous plants have grown sufficiently to smother them. Onions, perpetual spinach, sweet corn and tomato can all do surprisingly well in a sunny herbaceous border.

Growing in containers Containerised food crops can be grown on hard surfaced areas, so the total cultivated area of a garden can be expanded and production increased quite dramatically. Containers are also useful where the garden soil is below par, and worthwhile crops would be unlikely. Almost any pot, tub, planter, barrel or trough can be pressed into service, along with growbags. And if they are attractive and colourful, so much the better. The chief requirements are that they have drainage holes in the bottom and are large enough to hold sufficient fresh compost to sustain the crop. Plants in containers must be fed and watered regularly; any neglect will lead to reduced yields and quality. (See the table on pages 108-

109, 'Vegetables and salad crops', for suggestions of crops which will grow well in containers.)

Sprouting seeds The popularity of sprouting seeds as a boost to the diet is unquestionable, and you can have sprouted seeds ready to eat within four to six days of sowing, at any time of year. The method is simple and no elaborate equipment is needed. You can use a proprietary sprouter bottle, but equally good results are possible with an ordinary jam jar, a piece of clean muslin and an elastic band.

Wash a small quantity of seed inside a muslin-covered jar, filling and draining at least three times, then leave to germinate at 16-18°C (60-65°F). Rinse the seed thoroughly two or three times each day, and use as soon as the seeds have expanded to two or three times their original bulk.

Try adzuki bean; alfalfa; alphatoco bean; fenugreek; Chinese mung bean; or salad sprouts.

Grow mustard and cress in a seed tray, partially filled with peat. Sow the seeds thickly, moisten thoroughly and grow at 16°C (60°F). Cress should be ready to use in 15-20 days; mustard is a few days quicker.

Fruit

Choosing fruit crops Good quality fresh fruit can be grown in most gardens if a few simple rules are followed. The chief factors which influence the choice of fruit to grow, and affect subsequent success, are climate; available space; aspect; shelter and shade; and the state of the soil.

★ *Climate* Before you buy any fruits, find out which varieties do best locally. If you live in the north, or your garden is exposed, think twice before planting outdoor peaches or grapes; concentrate, instead, on hardy fruits.

★ *Space* Tree fruits need not be automatically excluded from small gardens, provided you go for suitable varieties

and forms. Wall-trained tree fruits, grown in cordon, fan or espalier form, need a minimum height of 1.8-2.4m (6-8ft). Cordon apples and pears can be planted 90cm (3ft) apart, while espaliers and fans need a wall space of at least 3-3.5m (10-12ft). Vigorous sweet cherries don't take kindly to retrictions nor to wall training, and are not well suited to small gardens.

Various berried fruits are suitable for training against walls and fences, as low as 1.2m (4ft) high. Bush fruits (black-currants excepted) are easily trained and grown as double and triple cordons. Raspberries can be planted near a wall but are best not actually trained against it. Rod-forming cane fruits like black-berry and loganberry are ideal for training over fences. Strawberries are small enough for most beds and respond well to container culture.

Apricots must be protected from frost and root dryness. The crop below is in good condition and ready for picking.

You will find most popular tree fruits are budded or grafted on to rootstocks of a vigorous, intermediate or dwarfing nature. Generally speaking, it is best to go for dwarfing rootstocks for small gardens.

Many tree fruits, including apple, pear and plum, are unable to set a good crop of fruit with their own pollen. To overcome this problem, either plant a second, compatible tree as a pollinator, or to save space buy a 'family' or 'Jenny'

tree. These trees have two or even three varieties grafted on to one root, and are self-pollinating.

In the table starting below are listed the most popular fruits for small gardens – with details of space needed.

Soft fruit for small gardens

Crop & Form	Distance apart	Aspect	Light	Notes
Blackberry Fan Tiered	2.4m (8ft) 3m (10ft)	S E & W	○ ◑	Needs rich, moist fertile soil. Stands light shade or a sheltered N facing site.
Black currant Bush	1.8×1.8m (6×6ft)	S & W	○ ◑ ●	Needs deep, rich moist soil. Tolerant of a N & E site if sheltered.
Blueberry Bush	1.8×1.8m (6×6ft)	S & W	○ ◑	Acid soil essential, moist and not too rich. Thrives in peaty conditions.
Gooseberry Double cordon Triple cordon	90cm (3ft) 120cm (4ft)	S & W	○ ◑ ●	Any reasonable soil, preferably high in potash. Stands shade.
Grape Double cordon	1.8m (6ft)	S	○	Likes fertile, limy soil and warm, sheltered position.
Loganberry	AS BLACKBERRY			
Raspberry Stool	50cm (20in)	S W & E	○ ◑ ●	Any reasonably fertile soil. Tolerant of shade.
Red/White currant	AS GOOSEBERRY			
Rhubarb	90×90cm (3×3ft)	N S E & W	○ ◑ ●	Needs deep, rich, moist fertile soil. Plant in spring
Strawberry in bed in container	45×75cm (18×30in) 25×25cm (10×10in)	S & W	○ ◑ ●	Needs fertile medium loam. Tolerant of shade and a sheltered N & E facing site.
Tayberry	AS BLACKBERRY			

Blackberry

Gooseberry

Strawberry

Tree fruits for small gardens

Crop & Form	Distance apart	Rootstock	Aspect	Light	Notes
Apple					
Cordon	90cm (3ft)	M9; M27			Reasonably fertile soil. Late flowering
Fan	2.4-3m (8-10ft)	M9; M26	S & W	○ ◑	cookers tolerate sheltered E or N
Espalier	2.4-3m (8-10ft)	M9; M26			facing site.
Cherry Morello					
Fan	3-3.5m (10-12ft)	Colt	W & N	◑ ●	Needs limy, deep, moist soil.
Peach/Nectarine					
Fan	3-3.5m (10-12ft)	Pixie	S	○	Needs limy, deep fertile soil.
Pear					
Cordon	90cm (3ft)	Quince C			
Espalier	3-3.5m (10-12ft)	Quince C	S & W	○ ◑	Best in fertile soil with good drainage.
Plum & Gage					
Fan	3m (10ft)	Pixie			Needs well limed, deep, moist, fertile soil.
Bush	2.4-3m (8-10ft)	Pixie	S & W	○ ◑	Culinary vars. stand light shade and a
					sheltered E or N facing site.

Cherry Morello

Gage

Plum

★ *Position and aspect* Planting against walls economises on space; while still allowing good crops. The direction in which the wall faces affects the crop being grown. South-facing walls, when unobstructed by trees or buildings, receive direct sun for most of the day. Being sheltered from the north, they provide the warmest sites. The south-facing wall is therefore usually best reserved for the choicest fruits – peach and grape in the south – or for dessert apples, pears or plums in cooler northern climates.

North-facing walls are shaded most of the time, and only suitable for a few fruits. Morello cherry, cooking apples and gooseberries are among those most likely to succeed. East-facing walls are liable to catch freezing cold easterly winds in spring, and are treacherous to early-flowering fruits. It is best to stick to late flowerers like blackberry.

Crop notes The following is a general guide to fruit cultivation. See the table on pages 118-119 and entries under individual names for details.

★ *Planting* Autumn is the traditional, and still the best, time to plant most kinds of fruit, especially bare-rooted trees and bushes. Container-grown plants can be successfully planted almost any time, apart from the depths of winter and the height of summer, when the ground is frozen, waterlogged or too dry. Be prepared to water, syringe and fuss over fruit which you have planted in winter, spring or summer, until it has become well established.

The ground should be free draining, deeply dug, weed free and well prepared. If possible, buy healthy ministry

certified stock of blackcurrants, raspberries and strawberries. Not all varieties are covered by the scheme, so ask your nurseryman's advice. Obtain ready trained tree fruits, to cut down delay in cropping.

Fix up wires, canes or trellis supports for tree and wall-trained fruits. Fruit trees can be planted quite close to walls; setting the base at least 25cm (10in) away from the wall should ensure no undue risk of damage to foundations. Plant tree fruits at the same depth as before the move. If setting them out in a lawn, leave a 30-45cm (12-18in) collar of bare soil around the trunk.

★ *Feeding and mulching* Most garden fruits benefit from an annual spring feed of general fertiliser – your nursery or garden centre can advise you. Apply at the rate of one to one and half handfuls per sq m (yd), spread over the root run and lightly hoed in. Water if the soil is dry before applying a generous 5cm (2in) layer of mulch.

★ *Crop protection* Net ripening fruits with bird-proof netting. Control pests and diseases – see pages 124-27.

★ *Pruning* See individual fruits for details.

Individual crops The following is a brief cultivation guide to fruit crops most suitable for the small-scale gardener. Tree fruits are dealt with first, followed by soft fruits.

★ *Apple* Summer prune cordons and espaliers in July. When new growths are about 25cm (10in) long, shorten them back to within about three leaves of older wood. In September, cut back all secondary side shoots to one or two leaves. Cut out the growing point of cordons every spring, back to the top wire, but not until the tip has grown beyond its allotted space. Prune bush trees in autumn. Remove crossing, dead and inward-growing shoots, together with any shoots which are causing overcrowding.

★ *Morello Cherry* These are best grown as a fan in small gardens. The fruits are

1. *Worcester Pearmain: a crisp, juicy, sweet dessert apple; both ripe and unripe fruit may be cooked.*

2. *Lord Lambourne: a crisp, juicy dessert apple with a good flavour. It can be picked from late autumn to mid-winter.*

3. *Cox's Orange Pippin: a dessert apple with an aromatic flavour. It can be picked from early winter to early spring.*

4. *Pitmaston Duchess: a large, late-autumn pear which can be eaten when raw, but is best cooked.*

5. *Williams' Pear Chrétien: a medium-sized, good quality pear; grows well on a north-facing wall.*

6. *Beurre Hardy: a large, late-autumn maturing pear of good quality; self-fertile.*

FRUIT TREES FOR SMALL SPACES

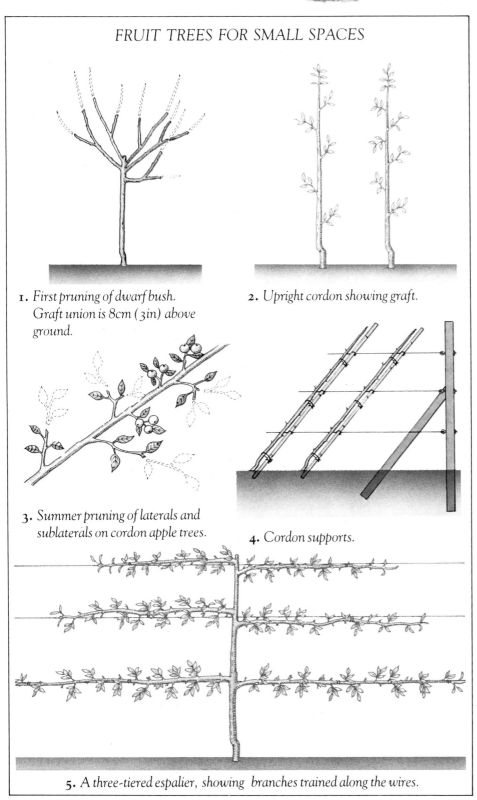

1. *First pruning of dwarf bush. Graft union is 8cm (3in) above ground.*

2. *Upright cordon showing graft.*

3. *Summer pruning of laterals and sublaterals on cordon apple trees.*

4. *Cordon supports.*

5. *A three-tiered espalier, showing branches trained along the wires.*

from above or down from below the main framework, to about 30cm (12in) apart. As these grow tie them in at about 10cm (4in) intervals. When these shoots reach 30-40cm (12-16in) in length, remove the growing points. It is these shoots which will carry the following year's fruit. (The following year allow one replacement shoot to develop at the base of each of these fruiting spurs [shoots], later stopping it at 30-40cm [12-16in].) The second stage follows after harvesting, in late summer. Cut out the fruited spurs (shoots) and tie in the replacement shoots.

★ *Pear* Treat as for apple.

★ *Plums and gages* In small gardens these, too, take up less space grown as fans, but this involves more pruning and training than when grown as bushes. Summer prune in July, shortening side shoots back to within six or seven leaves of the main frame. Subsequently, in September, shorten these back again, by about half. Thin them out to 10-15cm (4-6in) apart. These shoots will carry the following year's fruit.

★ *Blackberry* Cut back new plants to about 25cm (10in) above ground after setting out. As they grow, train the new rods either as a fan or horizontally to wires, to fruit the following year. Subsequently, cut out fruited rods to soil

Czar is a self-fertile plum for cooking; deep purple-red and a good cropper.

usually carried on shoots formed the previous year. Prune as for fan-trained peach.

★ *Peach and nectarine* Both these fruits crop on shoots formed the previous year. Pruning is carried out in summer, in two main stages. The first stage starts when the leaves unfold. Beginning at the top of a fan-trained tree, remove any shoots which grow directly towards, or at right angles away from, the wall. Next, thin out the shoots growing up

TRAINING RASPBERRIES, LOGANBERRIES & BLACKBERRIES

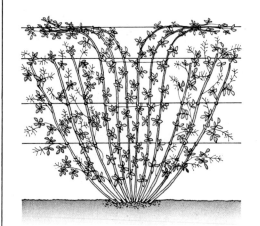

1. *Open-fan system (limited space)*

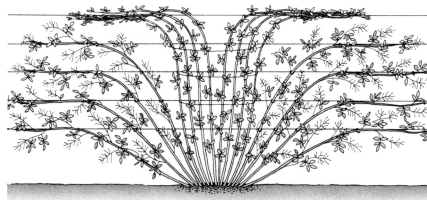

2. *Modified open-fan system*

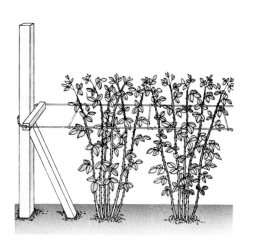

3. *Box system*

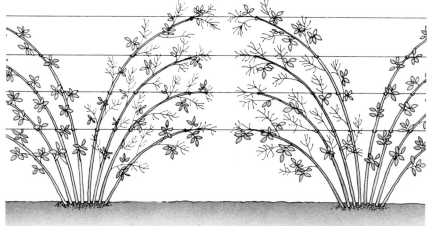

4. *Rope or arch system*

level as soon as picking finishes in summer, and tie in replacement canes.

★ *Black currant* After planting in autumn or winter, cut down bushes to a good bud on each stem, just above soil level. Subsequently, cut out weak shoots to soil level in autumn. On older bushes, aim to remove about one-third of all shoots each autumn. Remove the oldest first and take them down close to soil level.

★ *Blueberry* Lightly clip to shape in spring. Cut out crossing or dead shoots at the same time.

★ *Gooseberry* In June or early July, shorten all side shoots back to three leaves. The main stems of cordons are left untouched until they reach the required height, they can then be cut back annually.

★ *Grape* There are many ways to train and prune outdoor grapes. One method is to train plants up vertically, as double cordons, to about 2m (7ft) – tying in to wires or trellis against a wall.

In early summer, limit the number of side shoots to one per joint (i.e. the 'knuckle' or original leaf joint, which is now swollen). Pinch out the growing points at two leaves beyond a flower cluster, and at three leaves on the non-flowering shoots. Pinch out the secon-

The Riesling Sylvaner grape grows best in open ground and cloche-aided.

PRUNING GOOSEBERRIES

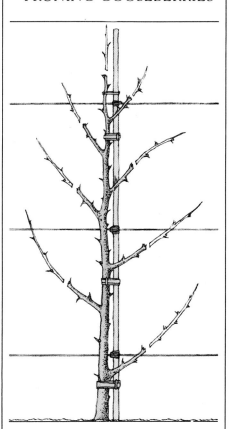

To prune a cordon in winter, the side shoots must be cut back to three buds.

LAYERING STRAWBERRIES

Peg the plantlet closest to the parent into a small pot of compost.

Pantagruella (above) comes in mid- to late summer and is acid-sweet in flavour.

dary growths at one leaf. In late autumn, after harvesting the fruit, cut all the side shoots back to a pair of buds close to the main stem.

★ *Loganberry* Treat in the same way as blackberry.

★ *Raspberry* Cut newly planted canes back to about 25cm (10in) above ground. With summer fruiting varieties, cut out fruited canes down to soil level, immediately after picking ceases. Thin out new canes to leave five or six per stool, cutting out the weakest. Tie in the new canes, about 10cm (4in) apart, to horizontal wires. Autumn fruiting varieties are cut down to soil level each winter in February, both the old fruited and new canes.

★ *Red and white currants* Treat as for gooseberries, except that the side shoots are summer pruned back to five leaves.

★ *Rhubarb* Stop pulling after 15th June each year, to enable the crowns to build up reserves for the following year. Remove any seed heads as they arise, and remove dead foliage in autumn.

★ *Strawberries* Clip off old leaves when picking ceases for the season, along with the runners which develop between the rows.

★ *Tayberry.* Treat as for blackberry.

PROPAGATING & PRUNING BLACKCURRANTS

1. Fruited shoots must be cut out at harvest time.

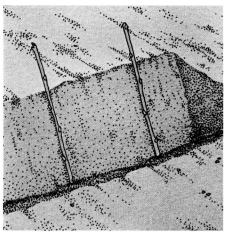

2. Cut-off shoots must be planted 15cm (6in) apart.

3. A bush must be planted 10cm (4in) deep and the shoots must be cut back.

PROBLEM SOLVING

Some of the most commonly troublesome pests, diseases and disorders are listed in these tables. You must beware of the various symptoms; the sooner you recognize a problem, and the quicker you act, the easier the solution is.

Common garden pests

Pests	Description	Treatment
Aphid (Greenfly & blackfly) Most garden plants come under attack. Aphids suck sap which weakens plants and spreads virus diseases.	Colonies of green, blue, black or pinkish insects clustered near growing points, on leaf undersides or stems. Leaves and young shoots curl and distort. Aphids secrete a sticky honeydew which usually becomes covered with a disfiguring sooty mould.	Spray at the first signs of attack with insecticide before numbers build up. Spray fruit trees with tar-oil winter wash to kill eggs.
Ants Ants build their nests among plant roots. Alpines and herbaceous plants in particular are loosened, wilt and die, if large numbers of ants are involved. Ants feed on the honeydew of aphids, and carry the aphids to fresh plants, to keep up supplies of their favourite food.	Scurrying black or brown insects are found beneath typical mounds of fine soil.	Use proprietary ant-killers in the form of baits, dusts or drenches.
Capsid bug These sucking insects damage a wide range of plants with a toxin as they feed on the young growths. Fruit bushes, trees, vegetables and herbaceous plants are all attacked. At first, leaves are spotted reddish brown, later holes develop as leaves pucker and distort. Buds are killed, fruits mis-shapen.	The tiny, bright-green insects are not easily seen against the foliage.	Spray with insecticide at the first signs of attack, drenching the soil around plants at the same time. Give fruits a tar-oil winter wash to kill overwintering eggs. Destroy rubbish in which the pest overwinters.
Carrot fly Seedling carrots wilt and die because their roots are destroyed. Grubs burrow into older carrots; in severe cases, the crop is ruined. Celery, parsley and parsnip roots are also attacked.	Tell-tale signs are a reddening and wilting of foliage. Small, yellowish grubs are visible.	Avoid thinning carrots, if possible; the smell attracts the fly. If this pest has been a problem, use a soil insecticide before sowing.
Caterpillars These variously feed on leaves, flowers, buds, shoots and stems of vegetables, fruits, flowers, trees and shrubs, leaving chewed holes. In severe attacks plants are stripped completely.	The grubs of butterflies, moths and sawflies are visible, in a variety of colours, shapes and sizes.	Inspect plants regularly. Hand pick caterpillars when numbers are small, or spray with insecticide. Clear up rubbish in which they overwinter. Spray fruit trees/bushes with tar-oil winter wash.
Cutworms This serious night-feeding pest chews through stems at ground level, so plants topple over as if cut off. Lettuce, young vegetables and annuals are vulnerable, but older herbaceous plants and annuals can all be severely damaged.	Large, fat, dirty-brown caterpillars are most active in early spring and late summer.	Cultivate the soil to bring the grubs to the surface, where birds will devour them. If they have been a problem, use soil insecticide before sowing or planting.

Pests	Description	Treatment
Leaf miner These grubs tunnel into the foliage of many plants; chrysanthemum, holly, carnation, celery, and lilac are most vulnerable. The shape of the tunnel varies according to the type of miner: blotches in holly, worm-like tunnels in chrysanthemums. The plant is eventually weakened.	Most miners are tiny, dirty whitish grubs, and only visible when the leaves are split open.	Control weeds, they provide shelter through winter for some miners. Spray as soon as seen; leaves can be hand picked in less severe cases.
Millipede These soil pests chew through roots, which is disastrous for small seedlings. Millipedes tunnel into bulbs and tubers, often taking over where slugs leave off.	Thin-jointed, hard-coated, up to 3cm (1in) long, sluggish creatures are found near the scene of the damage. They coil up like a spring when disturbed.	Trap in slices of potato buried beneath the soil. Clean up rubbish; control weeds. If this pest has been a problem, use soil insecticide before sowing or planting.
Red spider mite These are found on flowers and leaf undersides, and weave fine webbing over plants. Dry, warm conditions encourage them.	Minute yellow or red mites cause bronzing or mottling of leaves.	Spray, dust or drench with insecticide as soon as seen.
Slugs These feed at night, doing great damage. Above ground, they devour seedlings, older leaves, stems and buds. Below ground, they feed on roots, bulbs, corms and tubers, tunnelling into potatoes and carrots.	Slugs range in size from 1-10cm (½-4in). Those above ground are greyish black; those below ground are brown to white. Adults leave slime trails; young slugs don't, but are equally damaging.	Give regular applications of proprietary slug pellets or soil drenches. Clear up rubbish. Trap with fruit skins or beer. Make barriers or salt, lime or washing soda. Protect herbaceous plants with sand in winter.
Thrips These are sap feeders, sucking the leaves, flowers, pods and stems of most plants. Peas, broad beans, carnations, sweet peas, and onions are among the most vulnerable. Gladioli flowers and corms in store are attacked. Distortion is typical, as is streaking, mottling and flecking. Thrips spread virus diseases.	Clusters of active, tiny, long thin yellow to black insects are most noticeable in hot, dry weather from June onwards.	Watch leaf undersides and spray at the first signs of attack with insecticide. Dust gladioli corms with insecticide before putting into store.
Vine weevil Grubs feed on roots, bulbs, corms and tubers throughout the year, causing wilting and death in severe attacks. The beetles feed mostly at night, eating irregular holes in leaves. Indoors, pot-plants suffer; outdoors, strawberries, raspberries, rock plants, rhododendrons, camellias and clematis are vulnerable.	The beetles are a dull black; the larvae are fat, dirty-white grubs which, when uncovered, are usually curled up.	If beetles are seen, spray plants and drench the roots with insecticide, then work dry insecticide into the soil over the root run. Clear up rubbish to eliminate their shelter. When re-potting houseplants, hand pick the grubs and incorporate soil insecticide into the potting compost.

Slug

Red spider mite

Weevil

Common garden diseases

Diseases	Treatment
Black spot This common fungal disease of roses has become more troublesome in recent years, and is worst in wet seasons. Small, circular black spots appear on the leaves in spring and early summer. In bad attacks, stems are blackened. Premature leaf yellowing and drop are likely.	Pick up and burn all diseased leaves and prunings. Spray routinely, starting right after pruning in spring. use a suitable fungicide and follow the maker's instructions. If spraying is not a matter of routine, then start at the first signs of trouble.
Bulb rot Several diseases of bulbs, corms and tubers cause shrivelling, softening and rotting, with grey-blue or white mould growth in advanced stages. This can happen in store or while the bulbs are growing. Badly infected bulbs don't provide leaves. Leaves that are produced discolour and wilt, and flowers are lacking.	Only plant firm, sound, healthy bulbs, and set them out in fresh ground each year. Rest infected ground for five years. Give bulbs in store a dusting of flowers of sulphur or other suitable fungicide. Regularly inspect bulbs in store, and dig up suspect bulbs in the garden; burn any infected ones.
Damping off A disease of young seedlings, which causes them to topple over soon after germination. On close inspection, blackish/brown sunken stems at soil level are visible. Some plants can remain upright, but are likely to have wiry stems and a stunted growth. Damping off is worst in cold, airless, wet conditions.	Use disinfected containers and clean compost. Germinate at the right temperature, delaying sowing if necessary. Don't sow seeds too thickly. Water from below, and don't overwater. As a safeguard, colour the water the faintest pink with potassium compound.
Greymould This widespread disease attacks dead tissues and is troublesome both under frames and outdoors. Greymould is worst on badly drained soil, in cold, damp or humid conditions. Symptoms vary, but characteristically soft spots are followed by a more general decay, with a rapid spread of grey, fluffy mould.	Remove and burn all decaying leaves, flowers and fruits. Spray with a suitable fungicide at the first signs of attack, or spray vulnerable plants as a matter of routine. Strawberries and lettuce are very susceptible. Ventilate frames.
Mildew Mildews attack a wide variety of flowers, fruits and vegetables. They start in dry spells, then flourish in wet conditions. Leaves (often the undersides), buds and stems become covered with downy or powdery patches.	Don't overcrowd seedlings; cabbage and lettuce are particularly vulnerable. Spray with fungicide at the first signs of attack, then repeat as necessary. You can spray roses, gooseberries and apples as a matter of routine. Remove diseased shoots in autumn.
Rust Rust is most troublesome on flowers and shrubs. Rusty brown, orange or black spots appear on leaves.	Remove and burn diseased leaves. Spray with copper-based fungicide at the first sign of infection.
Virus Look for distortion, twisting and stunting of plants; streaking and mottling of leaves and flowers; and deformed outgrowths. Wilt and unfruitfulness are common symptoms.	Don't handle healthy plants after diseased or suspect plants before disinfecting hands and tools. Control aphids and other sap suckers. Buy Ministry-certified, virus-free fruits and potatoes if possible. Dig up and burn infected plants.
Wilt Clematis, asters, paeonies, carnations or pansies suddenly wilt and collapse.	Grow these plants in a different site each year, if practical. Dig up and burn all infected plants; re-plant new specimens elsewhere.

Black spot

Mildew

Rust

Fungicides/disinfectants

Chemical contained in wide range of proprietary products	Formulation	Use
Benomyl	Spray or drench	Systemic, useful for a wide range of fungal diseases including those on lawns
Bordeaux mixture	Dust or spray	Leaf spots, mildews and rusts. Don't use on seedlings
Bupirimate with triforine	Spray	Blackspot and mildews
Cresylic acid	Liquid	Disinfectant and soil steriliser
Dichlorophen	Liquid	Moss-killer and lawn fungicide
Iron sulphate	Dust or spray	Moss-killer and lawn fungicide
Potassium permanganate	Liquid	Soil and water disinfectant. Good for seedlings
Sulphur	Dust	Mildews, bulb rots and wide range of stem and foliage diseases
Thiophanate methyl	Spray, dip or drench	Systemic against club root, aerial and root diseases
Thiram	Spray	Good for seedlings and cuttings, against foliage and root diseases

Chemicals/pesticides

Active chemical in proprietary products	Formulation	Use
Bromophos	Granule	Pre-planting application to control soil pests. Useful, also, to protect growing plants
Calomel	Powder	Soil pests
Carbaryl	Dust	Caterpillars, weevils, beetles
Chlordane	Drench	Lawn pests, including ants
Cresylic acid	Liquid, spray or drench	Soil, tools and container disinfectant. Dormant tree spray
Derris	Dust or liquid	Aphid, caterpillar and red spider
Dimethoate	Spray or drench	Systemic against soil, stem and leaf pests, including aphid, red spider and thrips
Fenitrothion	Spray	Aphid, caterpillar
HCH	Dust or spray	Aerial and soil pests
Malathion	Spray	Aphid and most foliage pests
Metaldehyde	Drench or dry bait	Slugs and snails
Methiocarb	Dry bait	Slugs and snails
Pirimiphos methyl	Dust, spray or drench	Most leaf, stem and soil pests
Pyrethrum	Dust	Aphid, caterpillar and thrips
Tar oil	Liquid spray	Dormant tree/bush spray against aphid eggs and winter moth

In addition, there are problems which can be classified neither as pests nor diseases. They include:

Bud drop This can affect any flowering crop, and is usually due to a fault in cultivation.

Never allow the soil to dry out, especially during bud formation, and mulch generously in spring. Shade flowers against early sun and after frosts. Use a high-potash fertiliser.

Chlorosis This is due to iron deficiency and manifests itself as weak plants with yellowing leaves.

Treat with iron sequestrene.

Frost damage Ornamental and fruiting shrubs, leaves, shoots and flowers become black and brittle. Herbaceous plants turn soft and mushy, as do bedding plants and vegetable seedlings.

Cut back frosted shrub tips to sound wood; hand-pick frosted buds; protect herbaceous plants with straw, cloches or netting.

INDEX